CONTENTS

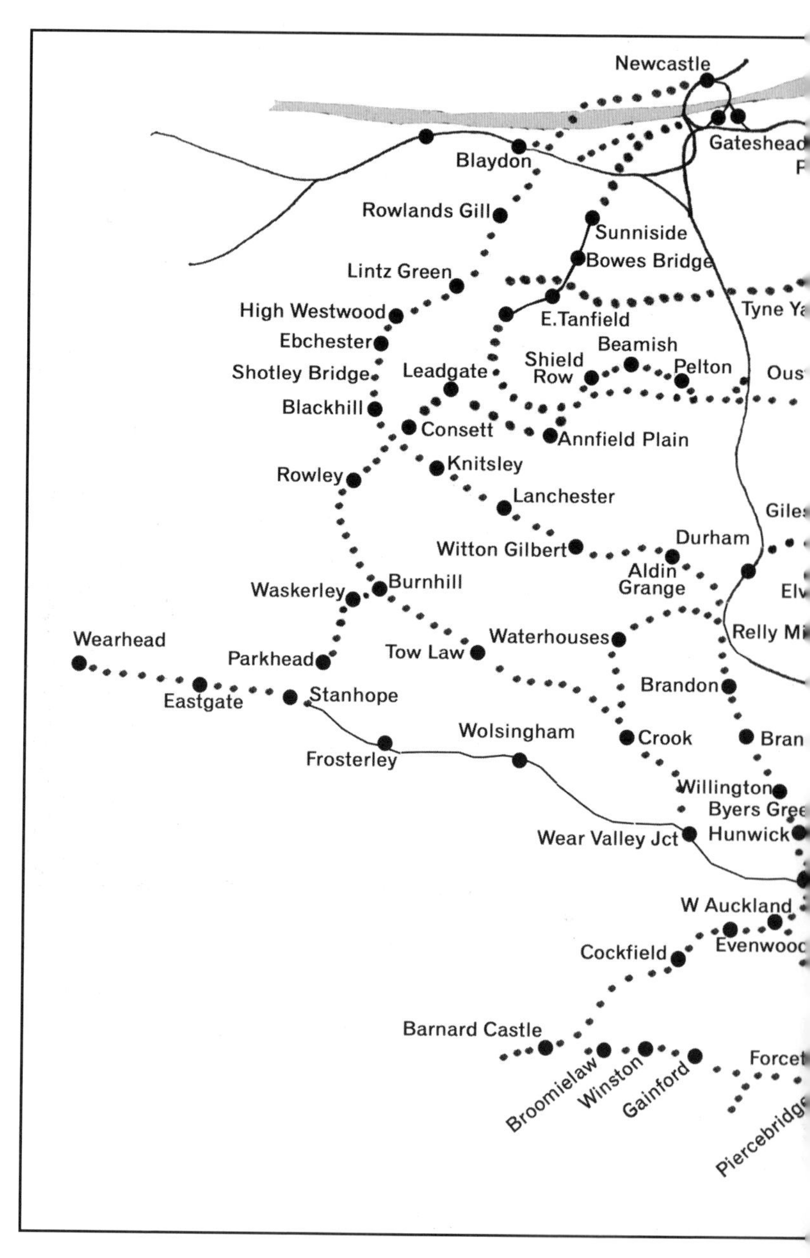

Newcastle
Gateshead
Blaydon
Rowlands Gill
Sunniside
Bowes Bridge
Lintz Green
High Westwood
E.Tanfield
Tyne Ya
Ebchester
Beamish
Shield Row
Pelton
Ous
Shotley Bridge
Leadgate
Blackhill
Consett
Annfield Plain
Rowley
Knitsley
Lanchester
Giles
Witton Gilbert
Durham
Aldin Grange
Waskerley
Burnhill
Elv
Wearhead
Waterhouses
Relly Mi
Parkhead
Tow Law
Brandon
Eastgate
Stanhope
Wolsingham
Crook
Bran
Frosterley
Willington
Byers Gree
Wear Valley Jct
Hunwick
W Auckland
Cockfield
Evenwood
Barnard Castle
Forcet
Broomielaw
Winston
Gainford
Piercebridge

LOST RAILWAYS OF DURHAM & TEESSIDE

Robin Jones

COUNTRYSIDE BOOKS
NEWBURY, BERKSHIRE

Cover picture by artist Colin Doggett
shows Frosterley station in June 1953,
with J21 No 65078 in action

Designed by Peter Davies, Nautilus Design

Produced through MRM Associates Ltd., Reading
Typeset by CJWT Solutions, St Helens
Printed by Information Press, Oxford

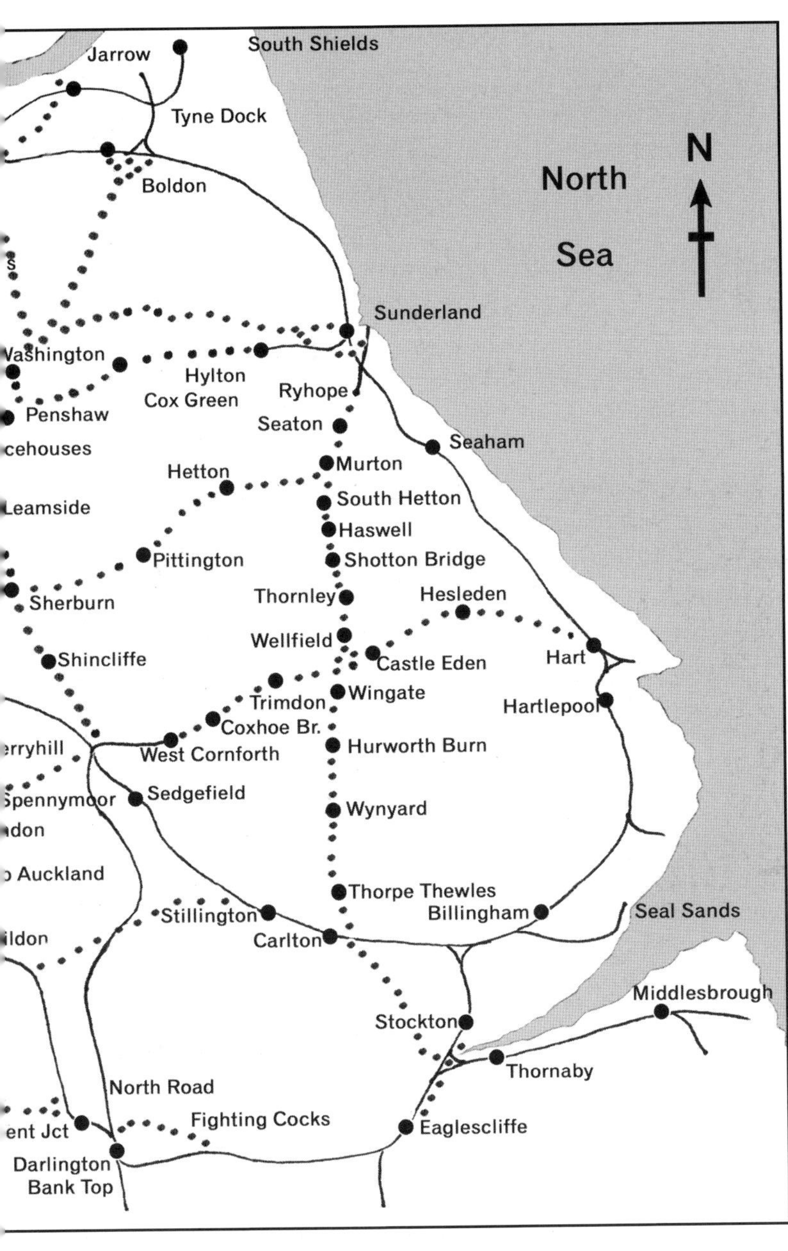

South Shields
Jarrow
Tyne Dock
Boldon
North
Sea
N
Sunderland
Washington
Hylton
Cox Green
Ryhope
Penshaw
Seaton
cehouses
Seaham
Hetton
Murton
Leamside
South Hetton
Haswell
Pittington
Shotton Bridge
Thornley
Hesleden
Sherburn
Wellfield
Shincliffe
Castle Eden
Hart
Wingate
Trimdon
Hartlepool
Coxhoe Br.
rryhill
Hurworth Burn
West Cornforth
Spennymoor
Sedgefield
don
Wynyard
Auckland
Thorpe Thewles
ldon
Stillington
Billingham
Seal Sands
Carlton
Middlesbrough
Stockton
Thornaby
North Road
Fighting Cocks
ent Jct
Eaglescliffe
Darlington
Bank Top

ABBREVIATIONS

The following abbreviations have been used in this book:

BARS	British American Railway Services
CR	Clarence Railway
DMU	Diesel multiple unit
ECML	East Coast Main Line
EVR	Eden Valley Railway
GNECHJR	Great North of England, Clarence & Hartlepool Junction Railway
LHJC	Lambton, Hetton & Joicey Colliery
LNER	London & North Eastern Railway
NER	North Eastern Railway
RCTS	Railway Correspondence & Travel Society
S&DR	Stockton & Darlington Railway
SDLU	South Durham & Lancashire Union Railway

Introduction

Durham could be called the birthplace of the steam railway. George Stephenson's Stockton and Darlington Railway pioneered the steam engine and from this beginning railway networks were set up all over the world.

It was the region's large coal industry which was the key to local development, though, with private systems springing up across the area, and a glance at any historic map of Durham and Teesside's railway system will give the distinct impression of a labyrinthine sprawl, without rhyme or reason. It will also seem that there were as many routes accessing the sparsely populated moorland areas as there were ones to urban centres such as Newcastle, Middlesbrough and Darlington. A modern map will look much simpler, with most of the region's tracks having been lost in the last four decades of the 20th century and now all that remains are the primary lines between the cities and the big towns.

The key to the pattern of railway development in Durham and Teesside was mineral wealth. For industrialists of the 18th and particularly the 19th century, the exploitation of the Durham coalfield was akin to a British version of the Californian gold rush. The development of the steam locomotive – in County Durham and Tyneside – paved the way for vast quantities of coal to be mined and taken out via Tyneside and Teesside ports, not to mention beginning a transport revolution that changed the world. A symbiotic relationship developed whereby Cleveland, and later Spanish, iron ore would travel in the opposite direction, leading to the development of new settlements like the boom town of Consett, which at one stage was served by lines from four directions.

Passenger services on these lines were almost an afterthought, the revenue that they earned coming a poor second to that from the transportation of minerals. Because access to mines, collieries and blast furnaces came first, the branch lines that enmeshed west Durham were not designed to go where people wanted or needed to travel, and so passenger traffic quickly fell as the motor car became widely accessible.

Thus, many of these railways lost their passenger services long before anybody had heard of Dr Beeching, some lingering on for freight purposes, until the exhaustion of the great coalfield meant that they had also reached the end of the line. The distinction between passenger and freight lines was often blurred from the start. A handful of routes that later became part of the national network carried passengers for only a few years. Conversely, there were many sprawling private colliery systems which had at various times run their own public passenger services, and which became part of the National Coal Board at nationalisation rather than British Railways.

Necessity is the mother of invention, and some truly amazing techniques were developed in order to export minerals, such as the series of rope-hauled inclines used by the Stanhope & Tyne Railway to overcome gradients in the days when steam traction was still in its infancy.

Durham's railway heritage is a testimony to human ingenuity. While much has been swept away, there is still much to see. Many of the lost railway routes have been converted to cycleways and long-distance footpaths, and those who use them will discover old stations, bridges and pieces of surviving infrastructure. In addition, there are several splendid museums: Beamish – the North of England Open Air Museum; Head of Steam – Darlington Railway Museum; and Locomotion – the National Railway Museum at Shildon. Through their extensive collections of key local artefacts these museums provide a gateway to the past.

Rediscovering the lost lines of Durham and Teesside, where so many groundbreaking innovations in the field of transport technology took place in the early to mid 19th century, is nothing short of retracing the roots of the modern age, which was shaped by the steam railway.

Robin Jones

1
Durham and the World's First All-steam Railway

County Durham did not invent the railway, or the steam locomotive, yet through a combination of both it reshaped the world. The county's unrivalled railway heritage stands as a monument to the great local pioneers who took a method of horse-drawn transport used for hauling coal trucks to the ports, and transformed it into a means by which continents could be shrunk, empires built and the fruits of the Industrial Revolution used to lay the foundation of our modern age.

Much of it has been lost, with the closure of mines and steelworks, the replacement of rail by road transport and the mass lifting of redundant lines. But although the county's coalfield and Tyneside in general may have long since ceased to be the great industrial regions that they were, there is still much that survives on the ground to remind us of the steam heydays long departed – the great days when Durham set the pace for the rest of the world to follow.

The railway concept has been shown to date back at least to ancient Greece, and some have said its humble beginnings were in use to move scenery on the stages of early theatres. The earliest evidence of a waggonway, the comparatively primitive predecessor of the railway, is the 5-mile-long Diolkos paved trackway, which was used to haul boats across the Isthmus of Corinth from around 600 BC.

Waggonways using wooden rails are known to have been developed in mid 16th-century Germany, while in Britain, mining entrepreneur Huntingdon Beaumont has been credited with building the Wollaton Waggonway in Strelley, Nottinghamshire in 1603–4, the first to be documented although some Shropshire lines may predate it. He also laid a waggonway near Blyth in Northumberland, kick-starting the railway revolution in the North East, and blazing a trail for others to follow ... in Durham.

The rich coal deposits around Newcastle-upon-Tyne had been known about for centuries, and the early historian, the Venerable Bede suggested that coal may have been dug there as early as AD 800. It was mined from seams at the surface around 1200, at first being used purely locally, and then exported from Newcastle-upon-Tyne from the middle of the 14th century. The port was ideal, because collier brigs could be loaded on the River Tyne before sailing down the east coast to the ever-growing market of London.

German immigrant cutlers and sword makers who fled from religious persecution in the early 17th century settled in the village of Shotley Bridge, near Consett. They are thought likely to have played a leading and significant role in the development of the steel industry in the valley of the River Derwent, which rises in County Durham.

Coal and steel were an explosive combination, as far as economic growth at the time of the Industrial Revolution was concerned. These raw materials paved the way for major industrial expansion, including the Tyneside shipping industry, which led the world in its own field, even building a complete navy for Japan in Edwardian times.

Needing fast and efficient means of transporting coal to its point of export, which in Durham's case were usually wooden piers or 'staithes' on the River Tyne if not the steelworks directly, waggonways provided the answer. Horses would haul rakes of loaded coal or 'chaldron' waggons from the mines and pits to the quayside. The waggonways were often designed so that they could complete much of the journey by gravity, the only control being a handbrake. Horses were used on the uphill gradients, and in several cases, a 'dandy' waggon was added to the train to carry the horses on the downhill lengths to give them time to rest before pulling the empties back to the starting point again.

A 'must see' for anyone interested in the lost railways of Durham is the Causey Arch on the original Tanfield Railway,

The Causey Arch, the world's oldest surviving railway bridge. Two tracks comprising wooden rails ran over it, and a horse and waggon would pass every 20 seconds in its heyday. A fire ravaged Tanfield Colliery, which the line over the bridge served, in the 1740s, and by the 1770s it was little used. (Author)

the route of which lies alongside the present-day heritage line of the same name. It lays claim to being the world's oldest working line, one of many railway superlatives proudly claimed by the county.

The oldest part of the first Tanfield Railway, the section in Lobley Hill, dates from 1647, and remained in regular use until the line closed in 1964. Like other Durham waggonways, the line was built to carry coal to the Tyne staithes. It was double track, used wooden rails and was constructed to a 4 ft gauge, and has been called the best known British waggonway of the period.

The preserved section of the freight-only railway, between Sunniside and Causey, dates back to 1725. Causey Arch, the world's oldest surviving railway bridge, was built to carry a new branch to a mine called Dawson's Drift. The bridge was constructed between 1725 and 1727, and at 105 ft long and 80 ft

A recreation of a typical Tanfield Railway waggon of the 18th century. (Author)

high, remained the biggest single-span bridge in Britain for another three decades. The Tanfield predates Yorkshire's Middleton Railway, which, authorised by an Act of Parliament in 1758, boasts that it is the world's oldest railway in continuous use, having been run as a preserved line since 1960.

Meanwhile, the big change to waggonways originated not in the North East, but in Cornwall, much of which was then also a heavily-industrialised landscape, where the smoking chimneys and giant beam engine houses of tin and copper mines were distinctive man-made features. The duchy relied heavily on steam technology to pump its mines dry, and it became a hotbed of innovation and technology. William Murdoch experimented with steam traction there, and ran a 19 inch long, three-wheeled steam carriage one night along the lane leading to Redruth church. It ran loose at 8 mph, terrifying the rector, who believed that the Devil was about to strike!

Richard Trevithick increased the level of steam pressure in stationary engines so that he could make smaller versions. He realised that if they could power a machine or pump, they should be capable of being adapted to drive themselves. This was the big turning point – the greatest since the invention of the wheel itself. Trevithick and engineer Andrew Vivian built a steam road carriage, which on Christmas Eve 1801 ascended Camborne Hill under its own power. Onlookers jumped aboard for a ride, thereby creating the world's first motor car. Trevithick demonstrated two steam-powered road carriages in London in the following two years, but they had one big problem, not of their making – the poor, bumpy, potholed roads of the period. The heavy road locomotives needed support – and so Trevithick looked to waggonways. In 1802, he built a railway locomotive for private use at Coalbrookdale ironworks in Shropshire.

Far better known is his demonstration on 21st February 1804 – for the first time in public – of a working steam locomotive on a horse-drawn tramroad linking Penydarren ironworks near Merthyr Tydfil to the Glamorganshire Canal. Trevithick is also said by some to have demonstrated or built an engine on the border of County Durham around this time. Christopher Blackett, the owner of Wylam Colliery in Northumberland, wanted a locomotive to run over a five-mile wooden waggonway built in 1748. It is said that a locomotive was indeed built, but was too heavy for the waggonway.

Trevithick's invention did not exactly spark off an overnight revolution, and many were convinced that the horse would never be replaced as the premier form of traction. His last documented locomotive, *Catch Me Who Can*, briefly ran on a circle of track in 1808 near the site of the future Euston station, offering the world's first passenger railway rides, but he made no money from his groundbreaking work, and afterwards gave up building steam locomotives. His invention was, however, by no means forgotten.

The Napoleonic Wars were placing a colossal strain on the supply of horses for British industry by the constant demand for horses to replace those killed in battle, and also pushing up the price of fodder, and so some mine owners took a second look at

The working replica of steam pioneer Puffing Billy *at Beamish Museum. (Beamish Museum)*

Trevithick's ideas. The Middleton Railway in Yorkshire upgraded from horse power to steam traction, incorporating many of Trevithick's ideas, and what is claimed to be the world's first commercial steam locomotive, the *Salamanca*, ran along it in 1812.

During 1813, engineer William Hedley, engine wright Jonathan Forster and blacksmith Timothy Hackworth built *Puffing Billy* for Wylam Colliery. The world's oldest surviving steam locomotive, and used until 1862, it is now displayed in the Science Museum in London.

The huge success of *Puffing Billy* led to demand for more locomotives for the waggonways of the North East, which accordingly became known as the 'cradle' of the railways, with the majority of Britain's waggonways being laid there. It also entered the English language in phrases such as 'puffing like Billy-o'. Beamish Museum, the best place in the world to discover and experience early railways and the industrial County Durham landscape of two centuries ago, launched a working replica of *Puffing Billy* on 13th July 2006.

Wylam was a pivotal place in the development of railways. It was the birthplace not only of early steam pioneer George Stephenson, he of *Rocket* fame, but also of Timothy Hackworth, his colleague, two dominant figures in Durham railway history and heritage. Stephenson designed his first locomotive in 1814, a travelling engine for hauling coal on the Killingworth Colliery waggonway in North Tyneside. He is said to have built sixteen locomotives at Killingworth, some of which were used on the first steam railway in County Durham – the first in the world to rely entirely on steam traction, with no horses in sight. This, the first of our lost railways, was the great turning point that had eluded Trevithick.

The opening of Hetton Colliery at Hetton-le-Hole and its associated private railway line on 18th November 1822 has been described as the most important event in the history of the Durham coalfield. The Hetton Coal Company, established in 1820, was the first significant joint-stock coal company in Durham. Its successful discovery of coal below a layer of magnesian limestone led to the opening up of the whole of the eastern area of the coalfield. The company was determined from the start to cut costs and boost profits by taking its coal directly to Sunderland to load into colliers, rather than following the example of neighbouring waggonways and run to the Tyne staithes from where keels would take the coal to Sunderland.

In 1819 the company took on George Stephenson to build what became known as the Hetton Railway. The construction of the 8-mile line began in March 1821. The biggest physical obstacle was the 636 ft high Warden Law, while at Sunderland there were steep cliffs down to the river. Stephenson's blueprint for the line, his first all-new railway, included two locomotive-worked sections, two rope inclines worked by stationary engines and five gravity-worked inclines. The first five locomotives were built by Stephenson between 1820 and 1822,

George Stephenson, who built the world's first purpose-designed steam railway in County Durham. (Author's Collection)

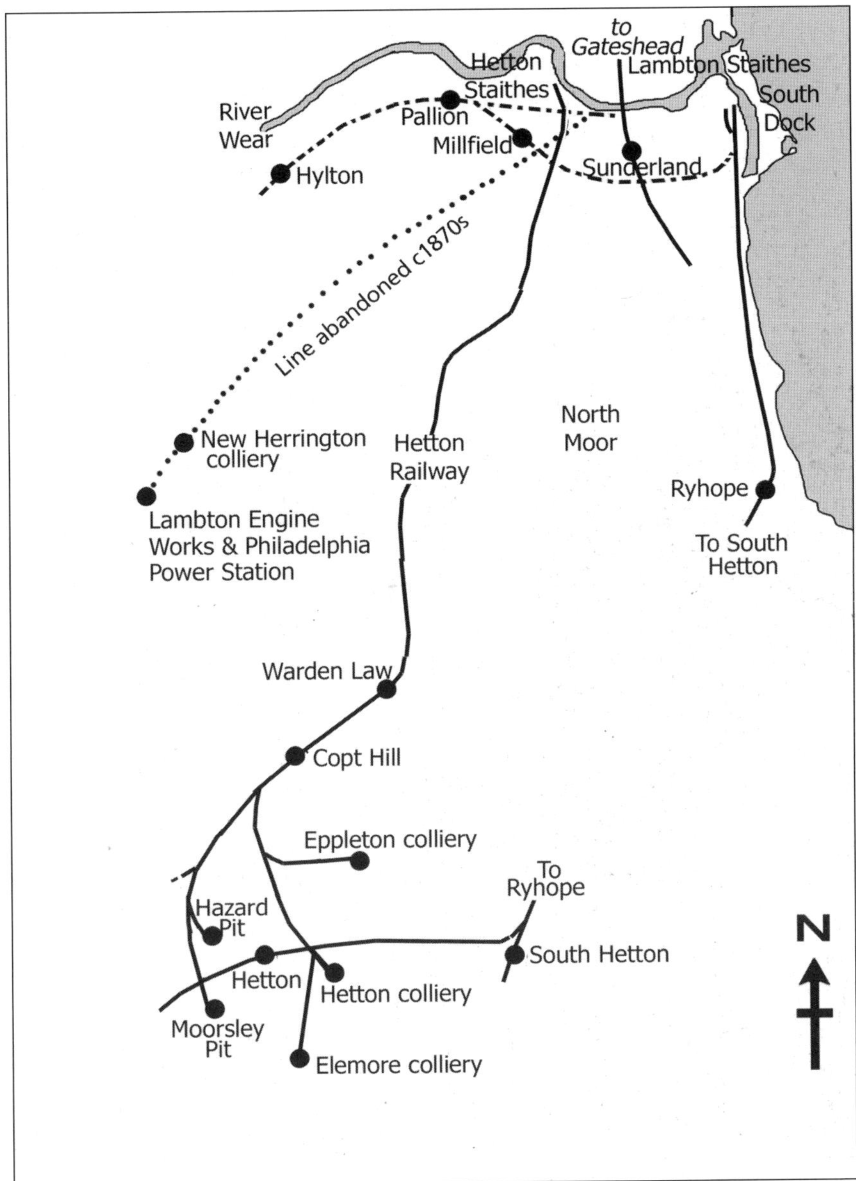

The Hetton Railway.

A contemporary sketch of Hetton Colliery, showing two locomotives at work. (Author's Collection)

all 0-4-0s with chain-coupled wheels, Four of them had names: *Hetton, Dart, Tallyho* and *Star*. The engine built in 1822 lasted in service until 1922, and is now preserved in the National Railway Museum at York.

At Hetton Colliery, extensive workshops were built for the building and maintenance of locomotives. Locomotive traction was not the whole answer at Hetton – far from it. A critical report published just eight months after the opening of the incline drew attention to the fact that on the final 1,533 yd length on the northern section, between the top of the staithe incline and the foot of No 4 incline, steam engines hauling trains of 16 empty chaldron waggons could not manage more than 3 mph – a speed that would present a major problem if coal production increased. In consequence, following the increase in traffic after February 1827 with the opening of Elemore Colliery, the locomotives were here replaced with rope haulage three months later, increasing the speed to 10 mph.

It is believed that one of the most unusual locomotives of all

The Hetton locomotive now in the National Railway Museum at York. (Author)

from these early days of steam railway development worked at Hetton. Built by Hawks and Company, a forgotten Gateshead firm of locomotive builders, the Steam Elephant was engineers John Buddle and William Chapman's answer to the iron horse. This oversize six-wheeled locomotive had a centre-flue boiler with two vertical cylinders set into its top centreline, and a colossal chimney. Trialled at Washington in County Durham, it was designed and built for Wallsend Colliery on the north bank of the Tyne. It struggled until the wooden railways were replaced with iron, and worked there until at least the mid-1820s. It may have then been rebuilt and used at Hetton for another decade. Records of it are patchy, and there may have been more than one Steam Elephant. However, that did not prevent experts at Beamish Museum replicating it from scratch

The replica Steam Elephant at Beamish Museum. (Beamish Museum)

The early 19th-century oil painting which helped provide the basis for a new set of engineering drawings to recreate a Steam Elephant. (Beamish Museum)

in a pioneering £360,000 project, producing a new set of engineering drawings from little more than an oil painting and four other contemporary illustrations. The new Steam Elephant was launched on Beamish's Pockerley Waggonway early locomotives demonstration line in 2002.

The Hetton Railway was rebuilt or modified in places on a number of occasions before Lord Joicey, the most powerful coal owner in Durham, added Hetton Colliery to his empire in 1911. The Hetton Railway then became part of his Lambton Railway, another private line.

The closure of the Hetton Railway began with its line to North Moor on 9th September 1959, after it had been decided to bring up coal from the new Hawthorn Combined mine at Murton Colliery. The beam engine at Warden Law incline was earmarked for preservation and dismantled; it is still awaiting reassembly at Beamish Museum.

The northern section between North Moor and Sunderland

survived the closure because the National Coal Board, which had taken over the line in 1947, had a contract to supply Sunderland's Hylton Road coal landsale depot, i.e. a depot where coal from a colliery was sold directly to the public for domestic use. However, the last coal from Hetton Staithes was shipped in autumn 1962. Subsequent piecemeal closures, including that of Silksworth Colliery on 5th November 1971, led to the final section of the Hetton Railway closing on 3rd June 1972, around 150 years after it opened. The track was all lifted by March 1973.

At Hetton, several workshop buildings survive, including some from the 19th century, such as the locomotive fitting shop, with its trussed roof and arched doors, which is now used as a garage. A commemorative plaque marks the cottage nearby occupied by Robert Stephenson when he came to live at Hetton in 1821, having taken over as resident engineer from his elder brother George. The later Lambton, Hetton & Joicey Railway waggon shop survives, with rails still set in the floor. Parts of the route between Hetton and Sunderland have been landscaped and much of it can still be followed, plaques not rails nowadays marking the route of George Stephenson's pioneering steam railway.

Four months after the construction of the Hetton Railway had begun, George was given far bigger fish to fry. He accepted the post of surveyor to the new Stockton & Darlington Railway, having first been approached by its promoter Edward Pease in April that year with a view to taking over the project.

2
The Stockton & Darlington Railway

Contemporary illustration of the official opening of the railway on 27th September 1825. (Author's Collection)

Four years before his *Rocket* won the Rainhill Trials on the Liverpool & Manchester Railway, its inventor George Stephenson achieved another world first in County Durham.

The Stockton & Darlington Railway was not the first railway in Britain. Neither was it the first public railway – that honour goes to the Llanelli & Mynydd Mawr Railway in Carmarthenshire, which began running trains in 1803. That was before the Surrey Iron Railroad, which is often and erroneously awarded that accolade because it was incorporated a few

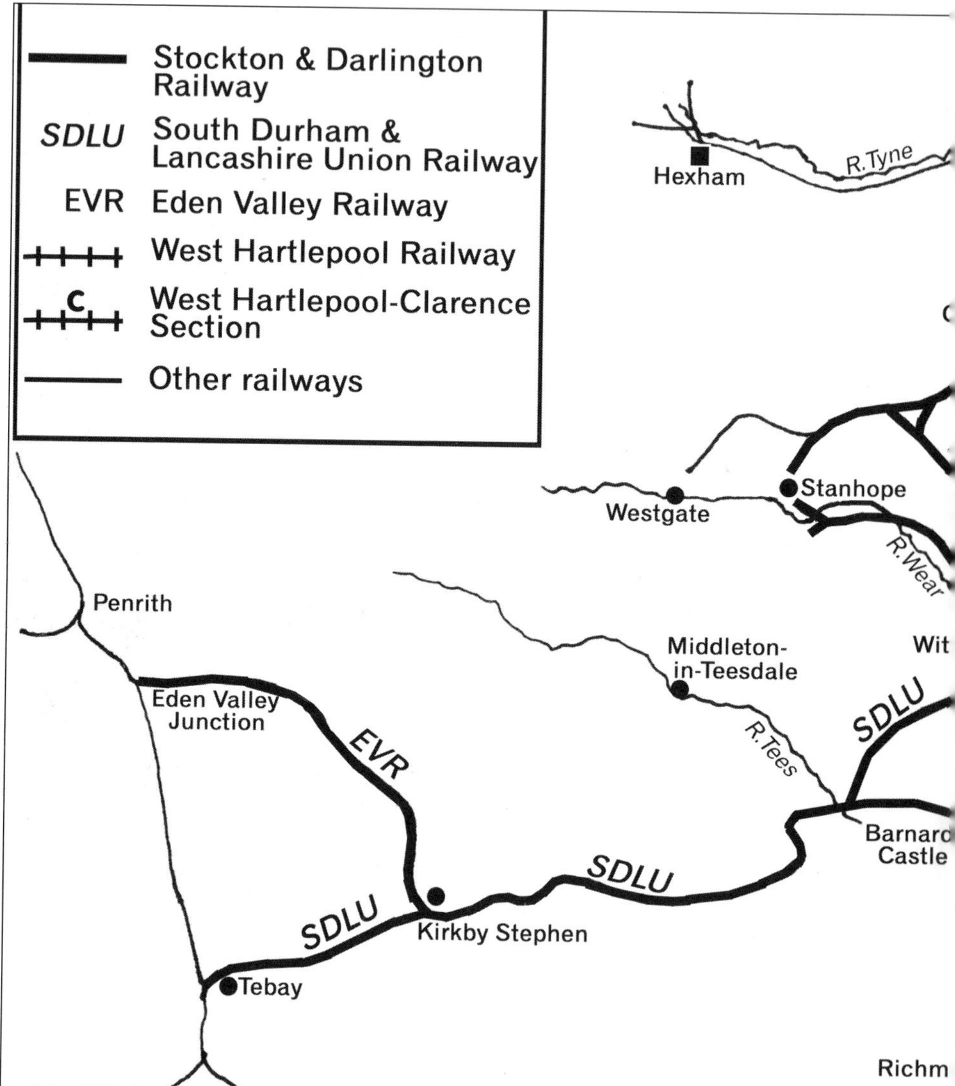

The Stockton & Darlington Railway and the South Durham & Lancashire Union Railway with its great Trans-Pennine Stainmore route, highlighting their position in relation to the Clarence Railway and the rest of the Durham network.

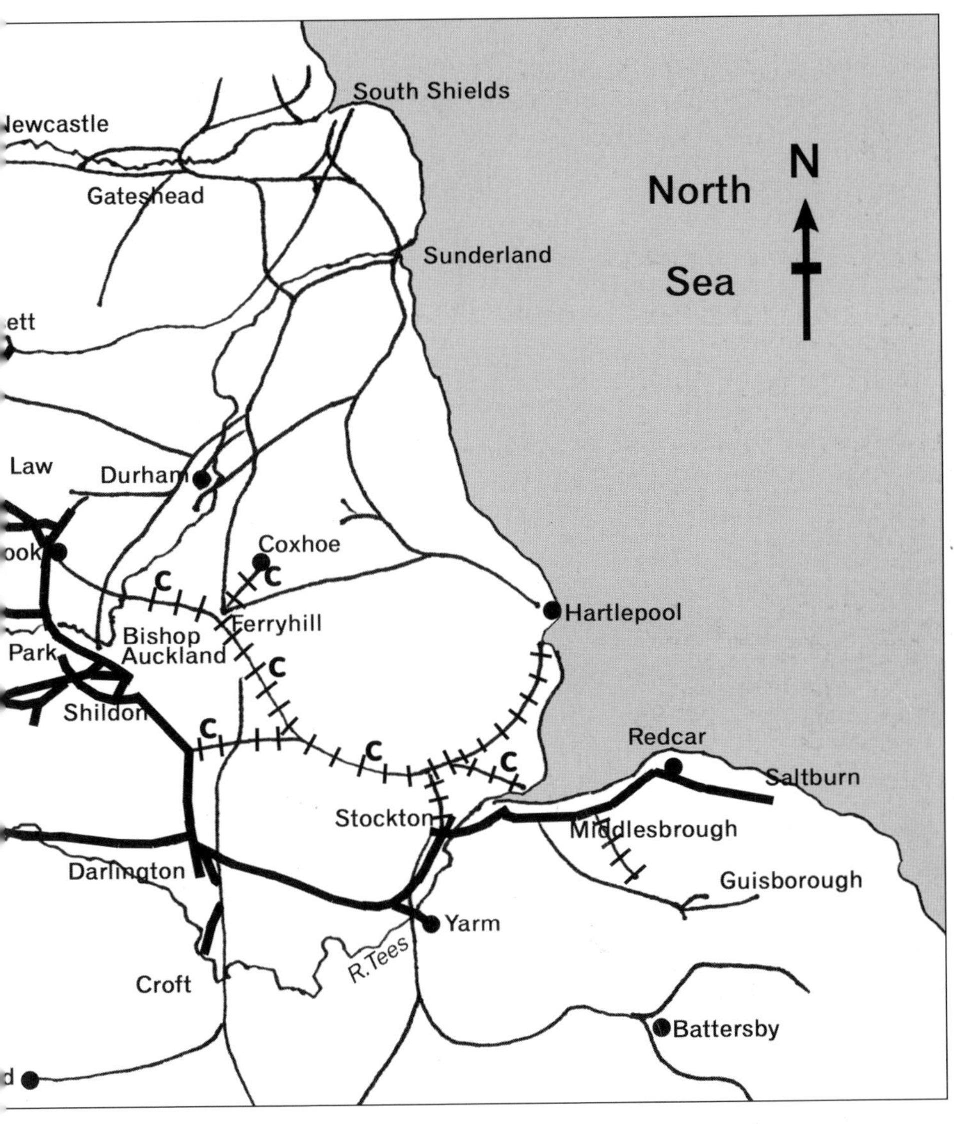
Newcastle
Gateshead
South Shields
Sunderland
North
Sea
N
ett
Law
Durham
ook
Coxhoe
C
C
Ferryhill
Bishop
Auckland
C
Park
C
Shildon
C
C
Hartlepool
Redcar
Saltburn
Stockton
Middlesbrough
Darlington
Guisborough
Yarm
R.Tees
Croft
Battersby
d

months earlier. Also, the Stockton & Darlington cannot claim to be the first public passenger-carrying line: that landmark was achieved by the Oystermouth Railway, otherwise known as the Swansea & Mumbles Railway, in 1807.

The big difference is that the Stockton & Darlington, which opened in 1825, was the world's first public steam-powered railway, insofar as it used steam locomotives to pull freight trains, as opposed to horse traction. It is often overlooked that its first passenger trains were also horse-drawn, and not hauled by steam. The Canterbury & Whitstable Railway, which opened on 3rd May 1830, provided steam-hauled passenger trains from the outset, and so predated it in this aspect.

The origins of the Stockton & Darlington lay in a scheme to build a canal to carry coal from the South West Durham coalfield to the navigable River Tees, where it could be loaded onto seagoing boats. In 1767 a committee met to initiate a survey. The great canal builder James Brindley appointed as surveyor Robert Whitworth, who the following year produced plans for a canal from Winston via Killerby and Darlington to Stockton-on-Tees, with branches from Thornton to Piercebridge, Darlington to Croft, and from Coatham Stob to Yarm, a total length of 33 miles.

George Dixon of Cockfield Fell Colliery even went as far as building a short stretch of canal in a bid to promote the scheme to the Earl of Darlington. He remained unimpressed and refused to advance any money, leaving the scheme literally dead in the water.

In 1810 Leonard Raisbeck, the Recorder of Stockton, proposed an enquiry into the possibility of building a railway or canal from Stockton, via Darlington and Winston, to the coalfield. Canal engineer John Rennie suggested a canal along the same route as Whitworth's.

Six years later, another proposal, this time for a canal from Stockton to Darlington and a railway from Darlington to a point near West Auckland, was mooted and in 1818, following a survey, the townsfolk of Stockton voiced their wholehearted approval. Leading members of the Darlington and Yarm communities, along with Leonard Raisbeck, had other ideas however, and met in Darlington on 17th August that year to consider building a railway. Wealthy local wool merchant and Quaker Edward Pease predicted that the railway would yield five per cent interest and he, along with some of his five sons and other members of his family, promoted the Stockton & Darlington Railway which by 1829 was being managed by Edward's son, Joseph Pease.

So, those at the meeting voted to apply to Parliament for an enabling Act, and a prospectus was issued. On 15th December, the Stockton party abandoned the canal idea in favour of the railway. Yet the two parties did not trust one another. The Stockton group considered that the line had been drawn via Darlington to promote the interests of that town, and were irate that tolls on the railway had to be paid for 30 miles even though the collieries were only 14 miles from Stockton.

The first reading of the Stockton & Darlington Railway Bill in 1819 was opposed by local landed gentry and was rejected in Parliament by a majority of thirteen. The scheme was revised, routes were altered and finally it was agreed that there should be a 26⅞-mile main line from Stockton to Witton Park and branches to Yarm, Darlington, Coundon and Haggerleases Lane. It was presented to Parliament in 1821, passed by the Lords on 17th April and received the Royal Assent two days later.

The line was intended to be open to the public, like a highway, on payment of the tolls of fourpence per mile for limestone, road metal, manure, coal, coke, cinders, stone, marl, sand, lime, clay and ironstone; sixpence per mile for lead, bar iron and timber; and a halfpenny per mile for all coal for export. A shilling per ton was to be charged for conveyance over the inclined planes on the route. On 12th May 1821, the new Stockton & Darlington Railway Company met in Darlington. Pease subsequently brought in George Stephenson who, later that year with his son Robert, resurveyed the route originally drawn up by Welsh engineer George Overton in 1818.

George Stephenson was appointed engineer on 22nd January 1822, at an annual salary of £660, minus the wages of assistants. It was Stephenson, hotfoot from the Hetton Railway, who persuaded Pease to opt for steam haulage. The formal inauguration of the railway took place at St John's Well, Stockton, when company chairman Thomas Meynell cut the first sod and laid the first rails 4 ft 8½ ins apart.

This in itself was an historic moment with global consequences, for this gauge, calculated by Stephenson from the average gap between the wheels of horse-drawn waggons of the day, soon became accepted as standard gauge for Britain's rail network and eventually for many of the world's railways.

In 1823 a second Stockton & Darlington Railway Bill was submitted to Parliament, asking for permission for deviations from the original line and for an additional branch line from Hill House to Croft Bridge. It also included a clause allowing for the carriage of passengers by steam power. It received the Royal Assent on 23rd May. One of the standout features of the railway was the Gaunless Bridge, designed by George Stephenson and built in 1823 in wrought and cast iron by John and Isaac Burrell of Newcastle.

Robert Stephenson & Company, set up by George's son Robert in Newcastle in 1823 to build steam engines, agreed to build a pair for the line at £500 each and provide two stationary engines, at Etherley and Brusselton for £3,482.15s. In 1825 Timothy Hackworth was taken on as the first locomotive superintendent. By this time, Stephenson was becoming very involved in the proposed Liverpool & Manchester Railway and was frequently absent from Tyneside, so he recommended Hackworth.

On 17th September that year, locomotive *Active*, later renamed *Locomotion No 1*, left Newcastle on a waggon drawn by a team of horses en route for Aycliffe Lane, later Heighington station. Once positioned on the track, the boiler was topped up with water and the wood and coal got ready to be lit. However, nobody had a light (it would be another two years before John Walker of Stockton invented the friction match) and so George Stephenson sent a messenger to Aycliffe to collect a lighted lantern. However, just as the messenger left, Robert Metcalf of Church Street, Darlington, who always carried his 'burning glass' (magnifying glass) with him so that he could use the sun's rays to light his pipe, stepped forward. He offered the glass to

Stephenson and by the time the messenger returned with the lantern, *Locomotion No 1*'s boiler was hotting up nicely.

The company's official coach, *Experiment*, was delivered from Newcastle on 26th September 1825 and attached to *Locomotion No 1* at Shildon before several directors, including Edward Pease and George Stephenson, undertook a trial run to Darlington. At 7 am the following day, 12 waggons filled with coal were taken from Phoenix Pit to the foot of the Etherley incline, where they were drawn up and lowered down to St Helen's level crossing. After a waggon loaded with flour was added to the train, it was hauled by horse across the Gaunless Bridge to the foot of the Brusselton incline, where some passengers, mainly labourers who had built the line, boarded.

A crowd cheered as the waggons were hauled up by the Brusselton engine and lowered down to Shildon Lane End (now Masons Arms Crossing) where *Locomotion No 1* waited in steam. From there, the engine hauled 21 waggons fitted with seats, along with *Experiment*, in the form of a procession led by a man on horseback bearing a flag. Despite two stoppages, the train reached Darlington inside two hours, having recorded an average speed of 8 mph. There, more waggons, including two carrying the Yarm Brass Band, were attached to the train, making a total of 31 vehicles, and 550 passengers set off to Stockton to a rapturous welcome six hours later. Sadly, Edward Pease did not attend the opening ceremony, as his son Isaac had died the night before. It was the first time that passengers had been officially carried on a public steam railway and earned the Stockton & Darlington an immortal place in the history books.

The name of the company was something of a misnomer, as Stockton to Darlington was 12 miles, much less than the overall length of the route. The only reason that Darlington was included the title was that the railway was mainly promoted by merchants from that town.

Hackworth went on to establish a locomotive works at Shildon and even built an engine, *Sans Pareil*, to compete with Stephenson's *Rocket* in the Rainhill Trials. *Locomotion No 1* suffered from a broken wheel soon after it entered service, and its boiler exploded, killing the driver, in 1828. The explosion

Derwent, an 0-6-0 constructed for the Stockton & Darlington Railway in 1845, is the oldest surviving Darlington-built locomotive, and is also part of the Head of Steam collection. (Author)

resulted in the locomotive being given a complete overhaul at Shildon Works, which allowed it to remain in service until 1841, when it was bought by Joseph Pease and partners for use as a pumping engine.

The Stockton & Darlington built a larger locomotive works at Shildon in 1833. Hackworth ended his connection with the railway in 1840 and continued locomotive building on his own.

The railway lasted 38 years before it was taken over by a bigger company, the North Eastern Railway, in 1863. During that time, through a series of amalgamations and takeovers, the Stockton & Darlington continued to expand in west Durham, opening lines such as the route from Shildon to Barnard Castle in its own name, and others jointly. The Bishop Auckland & Weardale Railway, which was opened from Shildon Junction to Crook, for instance, was leased and worked by the Stockton &

The sole surviving long boiler steam locomotive in Britain is this Dubs 0-6-0, No 1275, designed by Robert Stephenson and built in Glasgow in 1874 for use on the Stockton & Darlington Railway. It remained in service until 1923. In 2010 it was on static display in the National Railway Museum at York. (Author)

Darlington. In 1858 it took over the Wear Valley Railway as far as Frosterley, and then the Frosterley & Stanhope Railway in 1862 just before the NER takeover.

An extension of this line in 1845 from Crook to Waskerley was opened to serve as another outlet for the Derwent Iron Company at Consett. A line from Witton Junction (Wear Valley Junction) on the Bishop Auckland & Weardale Railway to Frosterley, with a connecting branch to Bishopley, was opened on 3rd August 1847, and in 1862 the Wear Valley line was extended to Stanhope by the Frosterley & Stanhope Railway.

The company extended way beyond County Durham, to Penrith on the West Coast Main Line via Belah Viaduct and Stainmore Summit on the legendary but long-gone Stainmore route. In 1830, Joseph Pease, who had now become the biggest owner of collieries in south Durham, was largely responsible for extending the railway over the world's first railway suspension bridge to a collection of huts further along the Tees from Stockton where new port facilities were created. This area became known as Middlesbrough and offered far greater potential for the expansion of shipping facilities. Three years later, in 1833, the Clarence Railway provided a shorter route for coal traffic from Shildon to the Tees and while sharing part of the Stockton & Darlington track, in several ways superseded it in this market. A statue of Joseph Pease stands at the junction of High Row and Bondgate in Darlington town centre. It was unveiled in 1875 to mark the Golden Jubilee of the opening of the railway.

A much-larger locomotive works was established at Darlington in 1863, and became the principal locomotive building establishment not only of the NER, but of its successor the LNER. It survived long into British Rail days and contributed many diesels to the 1955 Modernisation Plan.

The NER, created in 1854 by the merger of three major railway companies, owned the north–south route through Darlington, crossing the Stockton & Darlington on the level, while a new line from the NER's Bank Top station to Teesside duplicated much of the Stockton & Darlington route. Despite the fact that this new line became the main route between Darlington and Teesside, the Stockton & Darlington's east–west route remained open until 1964 for freight traffic. Afterwards, the short section from North Road terminated just east of the flat crossing over the East Coast Main Line for another three years, until it was also lifted.

East of Darlington, only two small parts of the original 27-mile route, Darlington North Road to Shildon and Dinsdale to Eaglescliffe, remain in use today as part of the national network, carrying a passenger service from Bishop Auckland. The remainder falls into the lost railway category.

As the first public railway, built before Britain was transformed by railways, the original Stockton & Darlington was inevitably largely superseded by later routes. Even where present-day rail uses the original formation, it is unrecognisable

St John's Well, No 48 Bridge Road, Stockton, was the original eastern passenger terminus of the Stockton & Darlington Railway and lays claim to being the world's first ticket office. The building predates the opening of the line and tickets were normally sold from local inns. It remains occupied, and the new Stockton road system has been built round it. The route to this point was kept open by British Railways for freight traffic until 1966. (Brian Sharpe)

as the original line, and many parts of the route have been completely obliterated. However, much of the heritage from the historic year of 1825 is still in existence.

With the heightened awareness of the value of the line's heritage, the original small Hackworth Museum at Shildon, set up in Timothy Hackworth's house, has been augmented by Darlington Railway Museum at the former North Road station, and the even bigger Locomotion – the National Railway Museum at Shildon. The first two are housed in genuine original Stockton & Darlington buildings. Locomotion, sometimes described as akin to a giant greenhouse but which nonetheless gives sterling service with regard to housing priceless items of the nation's railway heritage, is very much a 21st-century building that stands on the site of the S&DR marshalling yard.

Locomotion, an annexe to the National Railway Museum at

Timothy Hackworth's seven-bedroom house in New Shildon, next to the Stockton & Darlington works, was opened as a museum in 1975. (Author)

York, was built during 2004 at a cost of £11.3 million and was officially opened by Prime Minister Tony Blair. It houses locomotives, carriages, waggons and other artefacts not just from the North East but from all over Britain. The museum includes part of the site of Shildon waggon works, which had its origins in Soho Works, where Timothy Hackworth maintained the Stockton & Darlington's locomotives. The first engine built there was *Royal George* of 1827; amongst its innovations is said to be the blastpipe, which directs exhaust steam into the chimney in such a way as to draw the fire. In 1830 at the works, Hackworth built the *Globe*, hailed as the world's first specialist passenger engine, and first to successfully use cranked axles.

The Stockton & Darlington bought the works in 1855, and although it was closed by the North Eastern Railway in 1883, part of the expanded site developed as a major centre for wagon

The Locomotion museum in Shildon runs brake van trips along part of the original Stockton & Darlington route, to the Timothy Hackworth Museum. Visiting Manning Wardle 0-6-0ST Matthew Murray No 4 is seen passing the old coal drops at Shildon. The coal drops were a refuelling point for the steam locomotives. Wagons were hauled up an incline and the coal dropped down wooden chutes into the tender below. (Brian Sharpe)

building and repairs. One of the largest wagon works in Europe in 1975, nine years later it was closed after freight traffic on British Railways had fallen to the point where it was no

The redundant Hopetown carriage works at Darlington, which formed part of the original Stockton & Darlington Railway's workshops, is still playing a central role in steam technology, for the A1 Steam Locomotive Trust's £3 million A1 Peppercorn Pacific No 60163, Tornado, was built there, and is seen undergoing its first trial runs outside the building in August 2008. (Author)

longer needed. It too became a major part of Durham's lost railway heritage.

The Stockton & Darlington anniversary cavalcades

The importance of the Stockton & Darlington Railway lies not only in the field of transport technology but also in that of railway heritage, a sizeable player in today's tourism market. The concept of preserving locomotives for posterity dates back to 1839, when *Invicta* was withdrawn from Canterbury & Whitstable Railway and subsequently saved for posterity by Canterbury City Corporation. Incidentally, *Invicta* was the twentieth locomotive to be built by Robert Stephenson & Co of Newcastle, the nineteenth having been *Rocket*.

Trainspotting as a hobby for enthusiasts of all ages flourished in the mid 20th century, with hordes of schoolboys crowding station platforms, overbridges and other vantage points during weekends and summer holidays to log numbers of passing locomotives. Many of them later played pivotal roles in the railway preservation movement, saving locomotives from the scrapyard and reopening sections of closed lines on which to run them.

However, the preservation movement owes much to the most famous of all of Durham's lost railways, the Stockton & Darlington, for an event in 1875 changed the way the public at large viewed railway heritage. Early that year, North Eastern Railway director Henry Pease came up with the idea of holding an event to mark the 50th anniversary of the opening of a line with which his family had been long associated. It was decided that 'an Exhibition be held of Locomotives and other Engines, commencing with *No 1* and showing progressively the improvements made from the earliest up to the present time' at North Road Engine Works, Darlington.

The landmark event consisted of the unveiling of the statue of Joseph Pease, the first Stockton & Darlington treasurer, the presentation of a portrait of him to the Darlington Corporation, a celebratory banquet, excursions to places of industrial, topographical or antiquarian interest around Darlington and, most significantly, an exhibition of locomotives, which opened at the works on 27th September 1875. The anniversary day was declared a general holiday and shops and houses in Darlington were decorated by the tradesmen and citizens. Banners were hung throughout the town, including one that read 'The Locomotive, the Source of England's Greatness'. Bank Top and North Road stations were both decorated with furze, laurel and flowers, to greet the crowds that surged into the town on packed trains.

The original Locomotion No 1, *now on static display in Head of Steam – Darlington Railway Museum. (Author)*

North Eastern Railway chairman George Leeman led a VIP party round the works. *Locomotion No 1* was specially moved into the works from its pedestal at North Road station, and with the wheels raised above the track was supplied with steam so that the visitors could watch the wheels turn and the valve gear operate. Henry Pease stood on *Locomotion* and made a speech. Amongst the locomotives present was *Invicta*.

In 1925 the LNER marked the centenary of the Stockton & Darlington Railway with a far bigger event in the presence of the Duke and Duchess of York, the future King George VI and the Queen Mother, and 250,000 spectators, with the biggest-ever cavalcade of locomotives held to date, at Shildon. Although the actual centenary date was 27th September, the giant procession – comprising 53 locomotives and trains, old and new – was held on 2nd July 1925, to coincide with the meeting in Britain of the International Railway Congress, attended by delegates from all over the world.

An exhibition of locomotives, rolling stock and railway equipment was opened at the newly-completed Faverdale waggonworks at Darlington, while a large covered grandstand was erected at milepost 6 on the north side of the Darlington to Eaglescliffe line between the Goosepool and Urlay Nook signalboxes – on the same stretch of line where *Locomotion No 1* made its historic first run on 27th September 1825.

At 9.54 am on the big day, the signal was given for the first exhibit – the Hetton Colliery locomotive of 1822 – to move off under its own steam and lead the great procession over the main line. After the event, many of the older engines that featured were taken to York to form the nucleus of Britain's first dedicated railway museum, under the direction of the LNER, thus laying the foundations for today's multiple award-winning National Railway Museum and its Locomotion annexe.

To mark the 150th anniversary in August 1975, another grand cavalcade exhibition of locomotives and rolling stock and other relics took place at Shildon. For continuity purposes, the principal guest was William Stephen Ian Whitelaw, grandson of William Whitelaw, chairman of the LNER at the time of the 1925 cavalcade. Steam engines travelled from across Britain to

Beamish Museum built a working replica of Locomotion No 1 *in 1975, for the Stockton & Darlington 150th celebrations, as the original was considered too frail to be steamed and take part. The replica is seen steaming past Heighington on 31st August 1975. (Brian Sharpe)*

Shildon for the event, which featured many steam engines that had been rescued by preservationists, alongside modern traction, including the prototype British Railways class 125 High Speed Train diesel multiple unit. Ironically, just as the Stockton & Darlington set a benchmark in global railway history, the High Speed Train went on to become one of Britain's most successful examples of motive power of all time.

For the 1975 event, the original *Locomotion No 1* could not be made to run again without extensive rebuilding, which would have wiped out its authenticity as a historical museum item, so a full-size working replica was built by the Locomotion Trust, a group of engineering training establishments. It is now part of the Beamish Museum collection.

3
Stainmore: the Lost Trans-Pennine Route

Ivatt Mogul No 46449 and a sister locomotive double head an ore train over Stainmore Summit in the 1950s. (Author's Collection)

Stainmore Summit at 1,370 ft is the stuff that railway legends are made of. The words conjure up images of the bleakest, highest of the northern Pennines, the backbone of England, in subzero January temperatures, with North Eastern Railway snow-ploughs fitted and waiting to tackle blizzards and snowdrifts that could block the line for days. The route was made famous by the British Transport Films' *Snowdrift at Bleath Ghyll*.

The Stainmore Gap between the upper Tees and the upper Eden valley is the highest and sternest of all the Pennine passes.

Yet until the early 1960s, it was spanned by a spectacular 64¾-mile railway, which effectively linked the east and west coast main lines between Darlington and Penrith. It was a stupendous undertaking, designed to bring iron ore from Lancashire to the iron industry on Teesside and return coal and coke to Lancashire.

As described in the last chapter, the Stockton & Darlington Railway had its roots in a suggestion made in 1767 for a canal, which would run as far west as Barnard Castle. The canal failed to materialise, and when the Stockton & Darlington was built, it ran nowhere near Barnard Castle, to the disappointment of townsfolk, who on 1st November 1832 called a meeting to discuss the possibility of being served by a branch line. The problem was not the hilly terrain, but the stubbornness of the first and then the second Duke of Cleveland who did not want a railway anywhere near their land.

Initial plans were for a line running from West Auckland to Barnard Castle, but for the Dukes this was by far the worst option, as it would have cut their estate down the middle. The planned route was changed to run from Darlington to Barnard Castle, but the second Duke still opposed it. A Parliamentary Bill was defeated in 1853, but a second was successful the following year and the enabling Act was granted.

At a ceremony on 20th July 1854, the first sod of the new railway was cut. The Darlington & Barnard Castle Railway was opened in July 1856, and ran from a junction with the Stockton & Darlington main line at Hopetown near Darlington North Road to a station in Barnard Castle. The new railway was for local traffic only, but subsequent extensions gave it regional and even national significance.

While there was no local traffic to be gained from the moors to the west of Barnard Castle, in the 1840s several schemes were drawn up to extend the line over the Pennines to provide a new through route to the Lancaster & Carlisle Railway, joining it either at Tebay, or Clifton to the south of Penrith. These included the Yorkshire & Glasgow Union Railway, which would have run between Clifton and Thirsk, the Northumberland & Lancashire Junction Railway, which would have used the railway to link

Newcastle-upon-Tyne to Tebay, the Leeds & Carlisle Railway joining Leeds to Clifton, and the York & Carlisle Railway linking Bishop Auckland and Tebay and York and Clifton.

The Yorkshire & Glasgow Union and the York & Carlisle came together under the banner of the Northern Counties Union Railway and obtained an Act in 1846, but after building a few earthworks, ceased operations in 1849. Cumberland and Westmorland remained, however, crying out for a link with industrial County Durham, and in 1856 a meeting in Kirkby Stephen led to the formation of the South Durham & Lancashire Union Railway.

A blueprint for the South Durham & Lancashire Union Railway, running from Bishop Auckland to Barnard Castle, Kirkby Stephen and Tebay, was drawn up. It was decided to build the section from Barnard Castle to Tebay first, as it was already possible to travel by rail from Bishop Auckland to Darlington. In 1857 the enabling Bill sailed through Parliament in 1857 without opposition and the Duke of Cleveland, who along with his father had fought Darlington & Barnard Castle Railway, cut the first sod on 25th August 1857.

Without the benefit of anything like today's modern machinery, and having to chip away at the moorland with just picks and shovels, often in the harshest of climates, it took navvies nearly four years to build the 35 miles from Barnard Castle to Tebay, with many major extensive engineering works needed on the way. Two great iron viaducts were built, one at Belah, which was 1,040 ft long and 196 ft high, and a second at Deepdale, which was 740 ft long and 161 ft high. An iron girder bridge 732 ft long and 132 ft high crossed the River Tees. In addition, there were significant stone bridges at Hatygill, Merrygill, Mousegill, Percy Beck, Podgill and Smardale.

The line between Barnard Castle and Tebay opened on 4th July 1861 with intermediate stations at Lartington, Bowes, Barras, Kirkby Stephen, Ravenstonedale and Gaisgill and became a vital artery for freight traffic. Coke produced in County Durham ovens went to Cumbria for ironmaking at Barrow, Maryport, Millom and Workington works. In return, the superb quality haematite ore of the Barrow area was

The stupendous metal Belah Viaduct, one of Britain's greatest lost railway landmarks. (Stephen Middleton Collection)

despatched to the east coast where it was mixed with the poorer Cleveland ore.

It was the only line across the Pennines without a tunnel. While this pleased its financial backers, as tunnels were a costly engineering exercise, drivers and firemen were doubtless far less enthusiastic, as they slogged up the inclines that otherwise might have been avoided.

The building of the new line at first left Barnard Castle with two stations, because it was found to be impossible to extend the original line from Darlington beyond its terminus. The result was a long walk for passengers between the two termini. However, from 1st May 1862, the South Durham & Lancashire Union terminus became a through station, and the original town station was closed to passengers, but remained open for freight until 5th April 1965.

Although not itself in County Durham, a second operation that greatly increased traffic on the Stainmore line, the Eden Valley Railway Company, was formed in 1856 with the aim of

*The logo of the South Durham &
Lancashire Union Railway.*

constructing a route from a junction with the South Durham & Lancashire Union at Kirkby Stephen to a junction with the Lancaster & Carlisle Railway at Clifton. Building began on 4th August 1858 and the railway was opened for mineral traffic on 8th April 1862 and to passengers in June 1862. A junction with the Midland Railway's Settle–Carlisle line was laid 500 yards north of Appleby station.

Both the South Durham & Lancashire Union and the Eden Valley lines were worked by the Stockton & Darlington Railway from the start. That company formally took them over on 30th June 1862, just over a year before it became part of the North Eastern Railway on 13th July 1863. The remaining section of the planned South Durham & Lancashire Union Railway between Barnard Castle and Bishop Auckland opened to passenger traffic on 1st August that year. The line had intermediate stations at Cockfield, Evenwood and West Auckland, and the stupendous metal Gaunless viaduct which was 161 ft high and 640 ft long, spanning the River Gaunless at Lands.

Around this time, plans were afoot to build a line linking Barnard Castle to Alston in Cumberland, the southern end of the Newcastle & Carlisle Railway's branch from Haltwhistle. However, only the southern section of this route was built, by the independent Tees Valley Railway. It opened a single track 8¾-mile branch from Tees Valley Junction, a mile to the west of Barnard Castle just over the Yorkshire border, to Middleton-in-Teesdale on 13th May 1868, which from the start was worked by the North Eastern Railway. It served local quarries and much new stone traffic was added to the Stainmore line as a result, and

West Auckland station on the Barnard Castle to Bishop Auckland route. (Beamish Museum/K.L. Taylor Collection)

freight on this branch was always of greater importance than passenger trains.

With the rapid growth of freight traffic, much of the Stainmore route was doubled in stages from 1867–74 and the three viaducts were eventually rebuilt. By contrast, passenger numbers were always low, so much so that several of the smaller stations were for decades unable to run at a profit. While in 1910 there were seven trains between Darlington and Barnard Castle each way on weekdays, just three of them ran through to Tebay and Penrith, and by September 1961 just two trains ran from Darlington to Tebay each day.

The route was, however, used for excursions including summer Saturdays-only trains between Newcastle and County Durham and Blackpool. Also, an unpublicised service ran once every two weeks on a Friday, comprising a National Union of Mineworkers train from Durham to Ulverstone that took injured and sick miners to a convalescent home at Conishead Priory.

There were two minor branches between Barnard Castle and Darlington, running south over the border into Yorkshire. The private Forcett Railway opened in 1866 and ran from East Layton Quarry, Forcett Quarry and Forcett goods station to join the main line at Forcett Junction. It was closed on 2nd May 1966. Amidst hopes of great wealth being generated, the Merrybent & Darlington Railway was opened in 1870 between Archdeacon Newton to Barton Quarry to carry stone, and was closed in 1878 when the company went bankrupt in dubious circumstances. The line and quarries were reopened by the North Eastern Railway in 1890, but the railway was abandoned in 1938. The modern-day A1(M) follows part of the trackbed.

This coach is the sole surviving vehicle from the Forcett Railway. It was sold by the North Eastern Railway to the Forcett Limestone Company in 1884, and after ending up in the original York Museum, it was restored to its original identity as Stockton & Darlington Railway No 179 by British Rail Engineering Ltd for the Stockton & Darlington 150th anniversary event at Shildon in 1975. It is now in the Locomotion museum at Shildon. (Beamish Museum)

Stockton & Darlington locomotives worked the Stainmore route for the first three decades, and when the North Eastern Railway introduced its own 0-6-2 tank engines and 0-8-0 tender engines, stringent weight restrictions imposed on the viaducts meant that only smaller types could be used. Therefore the heavy mineral trains had to be double headed or banked, with a locomotive on the back as well as the front. By the 1940s, J21 class 0-6-0s were the primary locomotives in use on passenger trains, and J24 and J25 0-6-0s on goods. The weight restrictions were relaxed in 1954, allowing larger engines such as J39 0-6-0s on the summer excursion traffic. Soon afterwards, new British Railways Standard 3MT 2-6-2 tank engines made their appearance, but this was to be short lived.

The decline of freight over Stainmore set in after the First World War, firstly as more foreign ore was imported for the County Durham ironworks, and then as the demand for Durham coke in Cumbria dropped. Darker clouds began

Gresley V1 2-6-2T No 67765 hauling a passenger train along the Barnard Castle–Darlington line in British Railways days. (Author's Collection)

gathering over the route when the Tebay–Kirkby Stephen East branch became the first through section to close to passengers in December 1952, although occasional trains used it until 1961.

British Railways' Modernisation Plan of 1955 called for the replacement of steam locomotives by diesel and electric traction, and diesel multiple units and railcars were introduced on many rural routes in a bid to cut staffing levels and operating costs.

Diesel multiple units entered service between Darlington and Penrith on 3rd February 1958, and opened up the possibility of greater speeds over Stainmore Summit. However, despite an increase in passenger revenue, British Railways announced in December 1959 that it intended to close the entire Stainmore route between Tees Valley Junction and Merrygill, a mile east of Kirkby Stephen East, and from Appleby East to Clifton Moor. Disregarding a two-year public campaign to keep the route open, the Minister of Transport announced on 7th December 1961 that the closure was approved. The North Eastern and London Midland regions of British Railways shortly afterwards announced that the last trains would run on 20th January 1962.

The Railway Correspondence & Travel Society ran a steam-hauled special, 'The Stainmore Limited' that day, and it formed the final train between Darlington and Penrith over the Stainmore route, arriving back at midnight. The two locomotives heading it were British Railways Standard 4MT 2-6-0 No 76049 and Standard 3MT 2-6-0 No 77003.

As was the case with closures of lines in the 1960s, nobody thought of mothballing them for a time when economic, social and environmental circumstances would change – back in 1962 the term 'greenhouse effect' concerned only the growing of tomatoes – so track-lifting across Stainmore Summit began almost at once. All services between Barnard Castle and Bishop Auckland ended in June 1962. The line between Darlington and Barnard Castle remained open as part of the branch to Middleton-in-Teesdale, but the writing there was already on the wall. While the Stainmore route had not survived long enough for the Beeching Axe to fall on it, as it did on thousands of miles of the national network when the report *The Reshaping of British*

Magnificent Gaunless Viaduct, the 161 ft high, 640 ft span of the River Gaunless, which opened on 1st August 1863. Two years after the line's closure, the girders were removed and in 1966 the brick columns were dynamited. (Beamish Museum)

Railways appeared in March 1963, the Middleton-in-Teesdale service was an inevitable target for closure. The route between Darlington, Barnard Castle and Middleton was closed to passengers on 30th November 1964 and to freight on 5th April 1965, with the track lifted shortly after closure.

At Barnard Castle, the original station building still exists, as part of a residential development called Strathmore Court, with the front still appearing in as-built condition. The portico from the station was removed in 1863 and taken to the Valley Gardens at Saltburn-by-the-Sea, where it still stands today. The second station, however, was demolished following closure.

Sadly, the great metal viaducts were demolished for scrap, including Belah, at nearly 200 ft higher than any other in England, Deepdale, Gaunless and the viaduct across the Tees at Barnard Castle.

Near the western end of the Stainmore route, the six miles of track between Appleby and Warcop remained in freight use until 6th March 1989 and are now occupied by the Eden Valley Railway, a heritage project, which ultimately hopes to rebuild westwards to Kirkby Stephen East, where another preservation site has been developed around the restored station and offers short passenger rides. Some of the revivalists have expressed a wish to eventually rebuild eastwards towards Stainmore Summit … one day …

LNER No 4354 with a passenger train at Barnard Castle. (Beamish Museum)

4
The Weardale Railway, Crook and Tow Law

A lost railway found again: No 40 breaks through a banner at Stanhope station on 22nd May 2010 to mark the return of services to Bishop Auckland from the north. (Tony Griffiths/Weardale Railway Trust)

It took more than half a century to build the branch from Shildon to Wearhead. Early on, the Stockton & Darlington Railway planned a line to access the mineral wealth of Weardale, where ironstone mining had been active since the 1400s, and lead and silver mining boomed in the early to mid 19th century, with hundreds of mines active, not to mention numerous limestone, ganister, whinstone and sandstone quarries.

The railway promoters were reluctant to build a line across the moors from Shildon to Weardale because of the expense of crossing the upland terrain, so eventually settled for a stop-gap measure, the use of the Stockton & Darlington's short Haggerleases branch from West Auckland to Butterknowle which opened in 1830 and crossed the River Gaunless on a stone skew bridge. Lead from Weardale was taken by horse and cart to loading points on this branch, and conveyed from there via an incline at Brusselton to Shildon and Stockton. Silver for use by the Royal Mint passed this way too.

The Stockton & Darlington revisited the possibility of a branch in Weardale, as did the rival Clarence Railway. Eventually, a Stockton & Darlington scheme, the Bishop Auckland & Weardale Railway, which planned to run as far up the dale as Frosterley with an extension from Witton Park to Crook and a branch to Bishopley, was promoted in 1837, but only the line as far as Crook was approved by Parliament.

The seven-mile route from Shildon to Crook was opened for goods on 8th November 1843, with work on a temporary station starting the following month. An extension from Crook to Waskerley opened two years later to serve the Derwent Iron Company at Consett via part of the Stanhope & Tyne Railway. First known as the Weardale Extension Railway and later the Wear & Derwent Junction Railway, it had a rope-worked incline at Sunniside leading to a station at Tow Law and opened throughout on 16th May 1845.

In July 1845 the Wear Valley Act provided powers for the construction of a line from Witton Junction (Wear Valley Junction) on the Bishop Auckland & Weardale Railway to Frosterley, with the connecting branch to Bishopley, where limestone was quarried to serve the Teesside ironmaking furnaces. The branch from Bishopley Junction accessed the quarries of the valley of the Bollihope Burn and had gradients as steep as 1-in-47 and 1-in-43. These new lines were opened on 3rd August 1847, but the economic downturn of the day put paid to plans to extend the line further westwards into the dale.

When the railway opened to Frosterley in 1847, there were three passenger trains daily to and from Wear Valley Junction.

Stanhope station in the 1950s, with J21 0-6-0 No 65061 heading a passenger train to Wearhead. (Weardale Railway Trust)

It was not until 1862 that further progress was made, in the form of the Frosterley & Stanhope Railway, which, as the name suggests, extended the tracks to Stanhope and its large limestone quarries, while the Bishopley branch was also lengthened. One of the biggest was Parson Byers Quarry near Stanhope, which opened in 1872, high on the south side of the valley. It was linked to the Wear Valley line by an incline and was so big that it needed its own internal railway system.

Opening to Stanhope saw passenger services increased to four or five each way and one through to Darlington.

Still, the Weardale branch was not long enough to serve the numerous mining operations, with ore having to be brought to Stanhope by horse and cart. There were plans to extend the railway over the Pennines as far as Alston in Cumbria, joining the branch line from Haltwhistle, but the huge finance necessary was never forthcoming.

The last extension of the line comprised the nine miles to Wearhead, around 1,100 ft above sea level. It was opened by Joseph Pease, chairman of the North Eastern Railway, on 21st October 1895, and included the Greenfoot Whinstone Quarry, which had its own narrow gauge internal railway network, while the Weardale Lead Company at Rookhope was linked to the railway on the valley floor via an aerial ropeway. The extension bypassed the original Stanhope passenger station through which it was impossible to extend the line.

The Wearhead extension brought the total length of the line to 22 miles from Wear Valley Junction and 25 from Bishop Auckland. The well-equipped terminus included a single road engine shed (a sub shed of West Auckland), a goods warehouse, a turntable and a signalbox.

End of the line: J21 No 65078 on the turntable at Wearhead, possibly in the late 1950s. (Author's Collection)

The typical North Eastern Railway wrought iron footbridge from Howden-le-Wear now has a permanent home at Rowley station in Beamish Museum. (Author)

Between Eastgate and Westgate at Cambo Keels, sidings were laid to serve the Weardale Iron Company's Heights limestone quarry. During the First World War, German prisoners of war built a self-acting incline to link the quarry to the railway.

From the outset, there had been high hopes that the Wearhead extension would give a major boost to local mining, which was already seeing the start of a decline before the new terminus was opened, with the Teeside furnaces having turned to new supplies of iron ore from Cleveland and then from abroad. However, the extension never lived up to expectations, for the aftermath of the war and the 1920s brought about a sharp decline in quarrying in the dale, which at one stage had 13 miles of pits.

The Bishopley branch, which carried 25 million tons of limestone and lime during its existence, closed in early 1928, apart from a short section to Harehope Quarry.

One unexpected new source of traffic was the building of Burnhope Reservoir by the Durham County Water Board, for which Wearhead became the railhead for building materials until the project, authorised in 1922, was completed in 1936. The Second World War saw a brief resurgence in mining and quarrying, but it did not last.

The passenger journey from Wear Valley Junction to Wearhead took about an hour in each direction. Through coaches were attached to the rear of Darlington to Tow Law and Blackhill trains, and detached at Wear Valley Junction, where a

The last regular British Railways timetabled passenger train from Bishop Auckland to Wearhead in 1953. This train departed Bishop Auckland at 4.15 pm. There was a later train, which originated at Darlington and called at Bishop Auckland at 6 pm en route for Wearhead. It would have normally worked empty coaching stock back to Bishop Auckland after arriving at Wearhead but was given special dispensation to carry passengers as it was the last train. (Peter Wilson/Weardale Railway Trust)

branch locomotive, normally a North Eastern railway G5 0-4-4 tank engine, took them on to Wearhead. The station at Wear Valley Junction closed on 8th July 1935, after which trains ran straight through from Darlington to Blackhill and Wearhead. When Sunday services were operated, they ran only as far as Stanhope.

The branch would never pay its way on passenger uptake, and closed to passenger trains north of Bishop Auckland on 29th June 1953, a decade before Beeching. Until then, five trains per weekday served the stations of Witton-le-Wear, Harperley, Wolsingham, Frosterley, Stanhope, Eastgate, Westgate-in-Weardale, St John's Chapel and Wearhead.

Freight traffic to Wearhead was withdrawn in 1961 (the last engine based there being J21 0-6-0 No 65064), with the line being cut back to St John's Chapel in 1964, to Westgate in 1965 and to Eastgate in 1968. The railhead receded again in 1968, to Eastgate, where four years earlier a new cement works had reversed the sharp decline in the fortunes of the branch.

The Blue Circle, later Lafarge, works used purpose-built container waggons to transport cement to Teesside, Tyneside and Scotland. However, when the operation ended on 17th March 1993, the surviving 19 miles of the branch were mothballed. Rather than see the line torn up, local councils looked for an alternative use for it, and reopening it as a steam heritage line was the favoured option.

A revivalist company, Weardale Railways Ltd, was set up the same year, and attracted board members including pop producer Pete Waterman, railway publisher Ian Allan and botanist David Bellamy, although they later withdrew. The Weardale Railway Trust was formed as a voluntary group to support the company.

Little progress was made until local regional development agency One North East, Durham County Council and Wear Valley District Council pledged sizeable financial inputs. After the Manpower Services Commission agreed to help pay staff, a 40-strong workforce was recruited in 2004 for the new Weardale Railway.

It ran its first public services on 17th July 2004, using North

The 'Three Dales' railtour of 20th June 1967 behind K1 2-6-0 No 62005 at Westgate-in-Weardale station. (Weardale Railway Trust)

Eastern Railway P3 0-6-0 No 2392 and the Tanfield Railway's Austerity 0-6-0 ST No 49, topping and tailing between Wolsingham and Stanhope.

Within six months, however, it all turned to tears. Unlike other heritage railways, the project was run by a private company and relied heavily on paid staff rather than volunteers, and the initial operation proved unsustainable from income. The railway ran up debts of more than £1 million inside six months, and Weardale Railways Ltd went into administration on 2nd January 2005, with 36 staff laid off.

Despite the administration, the railway received the national Ian Allan Award for the best station restoration project of 2006 for Stanhope station.

Eventually, Ealing Community Transport, a London-based community interest company, took a 75 % stake in Weardale Railways Ltd for £100,000, and the railway's creditors agreed to a company voluntary arrangement. The line restarted operations, but again it would not last. Having attracted just 10,000 passengers in 2007 as opposed to a break-even figure of 35,000, Ealing decided to dispose of its railway division on economic grounds.

Weardale Railway resident steam engine No 40 in mock BR livery crosses Broadwood Bridge near Frosterley on 4th April 2010. (John Askwith/ Weardale Railway Trust)

Weardale Railway Trust-owned No 40, an industrial locomotive built in Newcastle by Robert Stephenson & Hawthorns in 1954, pauses at Frosterley station en route for Stanhope on Easter Sunday 2010. (John Askwith/Weardale Railway Trust)

A surprise saviour appeared in the form of United States outfit British American Railway Services (BARS), a subsidiary of Iowa Pacific Holdings, which acquired a 75 % holding in the railway from Ealing, with the Weardale Railway Trust and Durham County Council each having a 12½% stake. It went on to spend £1½ million in bringing the track up to standard, allowing services to be expanded from the previous Stanhope–Wolsingham round trips.

In September 2009 Network Rail reconnected the branch to the main line at Bishop Auckland, and on 19th February 2010, a diesel-hauled King's Cross to Stanhope charter operated by UK

The 1984-built class 141 DMU in Weardale Railway corporate livery used for the regular passenger services which began on 23rd May 2010. (Creative Commons)

Railtours became the first main line passenger service to traverse the line since the 1980s.

BARS does not see the branch as a heritage railway, but as a commercial line where freight will, as in the days of old, subsidise community transport. On 22nd May 2010 the railway's new timetable of seven-days-a-week, seven-trips-a-day public services using a class 141 diesel multiple unit over the 15½ miles of line from Stanhope to Bishop Auckland was officially launched, with heritage steam being operated at weekends. It is planned that the services will be subsidised by coal traffic, with the former Wolsingham steelworks site used as a loading depot handling coal extracted from a new UK Coal site near Sunniside. From Wolsingham, the coal will be taken to Drax power station in Yorkshire, reducing heavy lorry movements on the roads. There is also a scheme to build a rail freight terminal at Eastgate

The original station building at Wolsingham is now a private house. (Author)

for the loading of aggregates from local quarries, together with other freight, such as food and agricultural commodities.

Future expansion plans include running regular passenger services all the way from Eastgate, the current terminus of the 18½-mile former North Eastern Railway branch, through to Darlington, taking in Locomotion – the National Railway Museum at Shildon. A separate scheme to develop a 'hot rocks' eco village at Eastgate as a major 'green' tourist attraction is also seen as having massive potential for the line. There are no plans to rebuild the line west of Eastgate to Wearhead, its incredibly rich mining heritage all but consigned to the past.

At Wearhead, there is now a bungalow behind the former station building, the back wall of which has survived. The stationmaster's house is now a private residence. Elsewhere, along the Weardale Railway, original station buildings in places like Wolsingham survive, but are now privately owned and fenced off from the line, which is served by new replacement shelters. Nonetheless, it is a lost railway returned to the fold, and who knows – if it proves successful in its new incarnation, how many other lost railways of County Durham might be revived?

Crook and Tow Law

The opening of the railway from Shildon to Crook in 1843 and to Tow Law in 1845 gave local industry an enormous boost. Witton Park ironworks opened in 1846, importing Cleveland iron ore via the railway, and the Weardale Iron Company's works at Tow Law started operations the following year, taking ironstone from Stanhope in the opposite direction.

The temporary station at Crook was designed to be converted into railwaymen's cottages once a permanent one was provided. In 1846 a redundant platform from Stockton was sent to be used for the station. Opposite the station lay the Bank Foot coke ovens, fireclay works, chemical works and Pease's West Colliery.

One big hurdle that trains on the route had to face was the 1-in-44 gradient between Crook and Beechburn, the name of the station at Howden-le-Wear. In the earlier days, a stationary engine at Low Thistleflat helped locomotives climb the bank by attaching a rope, until more powerful locomotives made this unnecessary.

Crook received a second railway in 1858, in the form of the Stanley incline, which rose on a gradient of 1-in-16 from Crook to the Mount Pleasant stationary winding engine at 900 ft above sea level. On the other side of Mount Pleasant, this line dropped down to collieries at Wooley and Stanley. Initially, it connected with the Deerness Valley branch at Waterhouses (see Chapter 6). Although there were calls for it to be opened from Crook to Durham for passengers, this never happened; the line stayed freight only and the incline remained in use until 1961, just before Wooley Colliery closed on 2nd February 1962.

Tow Law station was first opened to passengers in 1847. A new route was built in 1867 eliminating the congested Sunniside

The Northern Football League was founded in 1889 and is the world's second oldest after the Football League itself, and in County Durham amateur soccer has always had a huge following. On 18th January 1951, Crook station was packed with supporters travelling to see the Shildon v Bearpark FA Cup tie. (Beamish Museum)

A5 class 4-6-2T No 69836 with a passenger train at Tow Law in British Railways days. (Beamish Museum)

incline, allowing locomotives to run all the way through to Tow Law for the first time, and a replacement station was opened in the town on 2nd March 1868. The four-mile deviation had a ruling gradient of 1-in-52.

The North Eastern Railway laid on a through service from Darlington to Tyneside via Bishop Auckland, Crook, Tow Law, Burnhill and along the Derwent Valley line through Blackhill and Swalwell. However, because the railway was far more suited to mineral traffic than passengers, people quickly switched to road transport when buses began running regular services, which served local mining communities missed out by the line.

One popular use of the line from Crook was pigeon racing, a sport that was highly popular amongst miners. A regular pigeon train was run for the local enthusiasts' association, an empty bogie pigeon van being loaded on Thursdays with baskets of birds. A locomotive would collect the van, add another to it at Bishop Auckland, and pick up more on the way to the West

*A Wear Valley goods train passing through Eastgate station. (J.F. Sedgwick/
Weardale Railway Trust)*

Country, where the birds were released by local station staff at a recorded time to fly all the way home to County Durham.

With a sharp fall in the carriage of lime and stone, the line north of Tow Law to Blackhill was closed to passengers as early as May 1939, ending through running to Tyneside. The Salters Gate Ammunition Depot was then built across the line between Salters Gate and Burnhill, all but closing the route, although munitions trains reached Burnhill station's transfer yard from either side.

The line north of Crook was closed on 11th June 1956 and passenger services between there and Bishop Auckland ceased on 8th March 1965. The line north of Wear Valley Junction was demolished within the next three years.

5

Leamside: the Lost Main Line

The East Coast Main Line, which runs from King's Cross to Edinburgh, is one of the busiest in Britain today, and indeed forms a backbone of the national network. However, when it was completed in 1850, and a banquet was held at Newcastle Central station to mark the achievement, parts of the ECML followed a very different route to the electrified main line we have today. One such section is the Leamside line in County Durham, which runs from Ferryhill in the south to Pelaw in the north.

The Leamside line came into existence in a somewhat arbitrary way when several shorter routes were joined up to form a main line. The first stretch to be used by passenger trains was that from Washington to Rainton Meadows, south of Fence Houses, in March 1840, having opened to freight in August 1838. This line was operated by the Durham Junction Railway, with expectations of a link to the Hartlepool Dock & Railway Company, but this failed to happen, and it left Rainham Meadows as the southern terminus of the route from Tyneside.

In 1844, the Durham Junction Railway became part of the Newcastle & Darlington Junction Railway, which had been initiated in 1841 by railway magnate George Hudson and aimed to connect both the towns in its title.

The northern section from Washington to Pelaw, incorporating part of the Stanhope & Tyne Railway, was joined with the southern sections to the south, from Rainton Crossing to Shincliffe and to Ferryhill. At Pelaw Junction, the line joined the Newcastle to Sunderland route. The biggest engineering structure on the line was the stupendous 10-arch Victoria Viaduct, which spans the River Wear and was so named because

Commissioned by the Durham Junction Railway, the Victoria Viaduct, which carries the mothballed Leamside line over the River Wear, was built between 1836 and 1838 to a Thomas Elliot Harrison design, based on the Roman bridge at Alcántara in Spain. (Peter Hughes/Creative Commons)

the last stone was laid on 28th June 1838, Queen Victoria's Coronation Day.

The completed route was opened to passenger traffic in June 1844, but as with many railways in Durham, mineral traffic was the main source of revenue, mainly in the form of locally-mined coal. The railway was served by several privately-owned colliery branch lines and waggonways.

The route became streamlined in 1849 when a more direct line between Washington and Pelaw via Usworth opened to freight, and was used by passenger trains from October 1850, doubling up as the ECML between Newcastle and Darlington, joining today's route to London at Tursdale Junction.

In 1854, the Newcastle & Darlington Junction Railway became

part of the North Eastern Railway. A new route from Durham to Newcastle was opened by the NER in 1872 and this is the section used for ECML trains today.

The Leamside line remained as an alternative route and for local stopping trains at the intermediate stations of Usworth, Washington, Penshaw (which was rebuilt in 1913 after being burned down), Fence Houses, Leamside, Sherburn colliery, Shincliffe and Ferryhill. Freight remained of paramount importance; at Washington, iron ore trains would be marshalled for the long haul up to Consett steelworks.

The first passenger closure came in July 1941 with the Leamside–Ferryhill service, while Leamside station was shut in October 1953. Leamside at one time had been a busy interchange station, with the line to Durham and Bishop Auckland plus a

In 1952, just a year before it was closed, racing pigeon owners were preparing to load their birds on to a pigeon van at Leamside station for conveyance to London. (Beamish Museum)

Timber being unloaded at the Co-op Wholesale Society furniture factory at Pelaw at the beginning of the 20th century. (Beamish Museum)

short branch to Durham's Gilesgate station running from Leamside (originally Auckland) Junction, but after closure it was completely demolished.

The Beeching Report of 1963 identified the Leamside line for withdrawal of passenger trains, but conceded it had a future for freight. All services between Pelaw and Fence Houses, along with the short western link to Durham and the Penshaw–Sunderland section, ended in May 1964, but several stations were reopened for one day in July 1965 for the Durham Miners' Gala, an annual event when special trains were run from pit villages, transporting miners, their families, bands and banners. The line remained in use for freight and also as a diversionary route, last being used as such during the electrification of the ECML.

Fence Houses station on the Leamside line on 27th June 1958. (Beamish Museum)

The gradual demise of the Durham coalfield in the 1970s and 1980s led to a sharp fall in freight traffic, and the line closed to all through traffic in 1991, following the closure of the Freightliner terminal at Follingsby near Washington. A short length from Pelaw Junction to Wardley remained in use for coal traffic from an opencast pit, but this has now also closed.

The line was not ripped up, as was the usual practice under British Railways, but mothballed, because of its potential to serve new opencast workings. The double track line was singled, with the track lifted at some level crossings, and the signalboxes at Whitwell, Fence Houses and Usworth were bulldozed in 1995, but Victoria Viaduct underwent extensive renovation from 1989–90.

An old steam era postcard view of Washington station. (Beamish Museum)

Mothballed it was, but will the Leamside line ever be returned to use?

Railtrack, the predecessor to Network Rail, in 2000 looked at the possibility of reopening it to freight to relieve congestion on the ECML. In 2006 Tyne and Wear Passenger Transport Authority commissioned a study into the line, with a view to possible reopening it for suburban services. Two years later, the study produced a report which said that the line would be best used for a regional service linking the Tees Valley and Tyne and Wear regions, cutting journey times between the two, as opposed to rebuilding it with a large number of intermediate stations. The report suggested that the best route for the proposed 'Tyne-Tees Express' would be the Leamside line and freight-only Stillington line. The stations would be Newcastle Central, East Gateshead (Park Lane), Washington Parkway (Glover Road), Washington (Station Road), Penshaw (Cox Green Road), Fence Houses (level crossing), Durham Parkway (Belmont), Ferryhill, Stockton, Thornaby and Middlesbrough. However, the report also stated that it was thought unlikely that Network Rail would upgrade the line for reopening.

Fence Houses signalbox, as seen in 1995. (Alan Lewis)

Durham County Council's Local Transport Plan also supports the reintroduction of passenger traffic on the Leamside line, and the Association of Train Operating Companies in 2009 listed Washington as one of a number of towns in the UK that would benefit from the reinstatement of existing rail links, either as part of the national network or as an extension to the Tyne and Wear Metro light rail tram system. In January 2010 the Tyne and Wear Integrated Transport Authority reiterated calls for improved links between Tyneside and Teesside to revitalise areas hit hard by the collapse of coal mining.

Despite fresh hopes for the future of the line, on 14th September 2006 Network Rail announced plans to rip up the mothballed track, arguing that after being out of use for so long it would need to be replaced if trains were to run again. A pledge was made, however, to keep all bridges intact and not sell off land that would be essential for any reinstatement project.

Lifting of the line had, in fact, begun in January 2003, when a mile of the track south of Penshaw was stolen over a six-day period by a gang of workers who were unaware that the work was illegal. A railway maintenance man hired a crew of casual workers who used JCBs, a tipper truck, lorries and floodlighting to remove the track – valued at £250,000 – in the hope of making £8,000 profit by selling it for scrap. He made the workers wear official maintenance jackets and paid them up to £50 a day.

The theft was discovered when a genuine member of a rail maintenance company's staff saw what was going on and raised the alarm. The man who organised the thefts was jailed for two years after pleading guilty at Newcastle Crown Court four months later.

Today, Mother Nature continues to reclaim the line by the week, with vegetation gradually enshrouding more of the rusting rails and rotting wooden sleepers, although the lengths with concrete sleepers remain sound.

6

Sunderland to Durham and Bishop Auckland

The Durham & Sunderland Railway
The Deerness Valley branch

A route from Durham via the Leamside line and Penshaw to Sunderland was opened by Newcastle & Darlington Junction Railway in 1853. As well as passenger trains, it was heavily used by mineral traffic to the docks at Sunderland, and linked to the extensive Lambton, Hetton & Joicey Collieries Ltd (later the National Coal Board) private standard gauge system. Unusually, the mining company's locomotives were allowed to run over the main line from the system at Cox Green Junction under an 1871 agreement, using the mile-long Deptford branch to reach Lambton coal staithes on the river.

At Sunderland, the line's original station was at Fawcett Street on a line leading to the docks, and just south of the present-day Sunderland station, which dates from when the North Eastern Railway opened a line from Ryhope Grange Junction over the river to Monkwearmouth on 4th August 1879. On the same day, Fawcett Street station and the Durham & Sunderland Railway's Hendon station were closed.

Beyond the first station at Millfield there lay Diamond Hall Junction, from where a short-lived line on the Queen Alexandra Bridge over the River Wear turned off on the right. The bridge, opened by the Earl of Durham on 10th June 1909 to link roads and railways running on the north and south banks of the Wear, was a financial disaster for the NER.

On the north bank of the river, the Hylton, Southwick & Monkwearmouth line, which opened in 1876 and served several mines, connected with the Stanhope & Tyne line at Southwick

The Queen Alexandra Bridge over the River Wear in Sunderland carried a railway for just twelve years. (John-Paul Stephenson/Creative Commons)

Junction, a mile and a half north of Washington. Before the landmark bridge was built, it was possible for rail traffic from the north to reach the docks at Sunderland only by reversing at Fawcett Street or Ryhope Grange Junction. The four-span bridge provided direct access via the Penshaw–Sunderland line to the docks. The NER agreed with Sunderland Corporation to share the £450,000 cost of the two-tier bridge, which was designed by the railway's architect, C.A. Harrison, and stands at 85 ft above water level. The branch over the bridge opened to freight traffic on 20th September 1909, but never saw passenger use. Useful the route certainly was, but the decline in coal traffic, which set in after the First World War, led to low traffic volumes. These decreased to the point where it was decided in 1921 to close the railway line over the bridge. The lower deck still carries the roadway while a water main is the sole occupant of the rail deck above.

Before Pallion station was reached by westbound trains, the abovementioned Deptford branch joined the main line. Beyond here, the Ford paper works was served by a rope incline as it lay below the level of the railway. There were two further intermediate stations, Hylton and Cox Green, before an end-on junction with the Lambton system adjacent to Penshaw North signalbox, and the junction with the Leamside line.

Just north of Rainton Meadows, the Leamside line was crossed on the level by the Lambton Railway, serving Frankland and Framwellgate Moor pits. At Leamside Junction, the Bishop Auckland branch left the Leamside line and ran over the nine-arch Brasside Viaduct to Newton Hall Junction, where it joined today's East Coast Main Line to run into Durham before diverging again at Relly Mill Junction South towards Brancepeth, Willington, Hunwick and Bishop Auckland stations.

Just south of Leamside Junction on the Leamside line was Belmont Junction, the start of a short branch to the eastern side

Willington station as pictured in 1906. (Beamish Museum)

of Durham where it had a terminus station at Gilesgate, opened on 18th June 1844. At the time it was Durham's main station for London-bound trains, via the Leamside line. Both Belmont Junction and Gilesgate station were closed to passengers on 1st April 1857 when the existing Durham station on what was then the Leamside–Bishop Auckland line was opened.

Gilesgate lived on as the Durham City goods station until its closure on 7th November 1966 was partially necessitated by roadworks. It now serves as a Travelodge hotel.

The 11-mile line from Bishop Auckland to Durham was built by the NER and opened to freight on 19th August 1856 and to passengers on 1st April 1857, the town's original Stockton & Darlington Railway station being replaced by a joint NER/S&DR structure on the present-day site later that year. As traffic volumes grew, particularly with the opening of the South Durham & Lancashire Union Railway branch to Barnard Castle and on to Tebay in 1861, it was rebuilt again in 1867 and 1905, the latter in an unusual triangular format. An additional station at Brandon Colliery, served by a private freight branch to Brandon Pit House Colliery, was opened in 1861.

The branch was also linked to many other mines including Hunwick Colliery with a line to Newfield Colliery and Brickworks from Hunwick station, Rough Lea Colliery, West Hunwick Colliery, Willington and Sunnybrow Collieries via a link to the West Durham Railway and Brancepeth Colliery, which had a private line to Oakenshaw Colliery.

The line also provided a diversionary route for the ECML when engineering works were in progress between Darlington and Durham. While it initially facilitated a passenger service from Bishop Auckland to Sunderland, it was later extended to Middleton-in-Teesdale to Sunderland.

Freight facilities were withdrawn from Hunwick in 1958. The Sunderland–Durham–Bishop Auckland passenger service was withdrawn on 4th May 1964, but goods lingered on for another four years.

The short length between Relly Mill Junction and Deerness Valley Junction, where the branches from Durham to Waterhouses and Consett diverged, is now part of the realigned

Prototype Tyne and Wear Metro train 4001 in original livery (cadmium yellow and white with a maroon stripe) at South Hylton station in 2005. (Chris McKenna/Creative Commons)

ECML, easing a curve to boost line speed. Virtually the rest of the line from Durham has been turned into the 9½-mile Brandon to Bishop Auckland Railway Path. The Durham platforms at Bishop Auckland have long since been demolished and the site is occupied by a store.

The line between Penshaw and the Ford works at Hylton closed to freight in 1967 and was lifted in 1970. The section of the route between Sunderland and South Hylton was relaid and reopened in 2002 as part of an extension to the Tyne and Wear Metro network. The new terminus at South Hylton has the longest platform on the light rail network and can accommodate two trains. The extension from Sunderland has intermediate stations at Pallion, Millfield, University and Park Lane.

The Durham & Sunderland Railway

The first railway to serve the county town of Durham had been the Durham & Sunderland Railway, not to be confused with the Newcastle & Darlington Junction Railway's route between the towns. At first rope-hauled, the initial section from Sunderland Town Moor to Pittington was opened in 1836. The line was extended to Sherburn House in 1837 and to the terminus on 28th June 1839, at Shincliffe to the south of Durham, not near the city centre. There were intermediate stations at Ryhope, Seaton Bank Top, Murton and Hetton. Beyond Shincliffe, a freight-only line ran west to Houghall Colliery. A further section from here to Croxdale Colliery was abandoned in the 1830s. It was not until 1857 that locomotives were introduced.

The Durham & Sunderland Railway was bought in 1846 by the Newcastle & Darlington Junction Railway, which obtained powers to build a line from the north of Sherburn to Shincliffe and on to Bishop Auckland. The Newcastle & Darlington had opened the first station in Durham city on 18th June 1844, with a branch from Belmont Junction to Gilesgate.

That year the Newcastle & Darlington Junction Railway became the York & Newcastle Railway and in 1847 amalgamated with the York, Newcastle & Berwick Railway. A succession of mergers in 1854 led to the creation of the North Eastern Railway.

The NER opened a station at Elvet in Durham in 1893, with a new branch linking it to the existing Shincliffe line at Sherburn House. From 24th July that year, Shincliffe station was closed and Sherburn House station moved from the junction onto the new branch. Passenger services to Elvet and Sherburn House were withdrawn as early as 1st January 1931, although the station remained in use for just one day each year, apart from during the Second World War, for the Durham Miners' Gala. In 1953 a travelling circus from the Continent arrived by train at Elvet.

The line from Sunderland to Pittington remained open until 5th January 1953 while the branch from Murton was used until

Sherburn House was the first station east of Durham Elvet. (Beamish Museum)

the late 1950s for wagon storage. The Hetton to Sherburn section closed to all traffic on 3rd April 1960 and the remaining part to Murton on 11th November 1963. A single track spur from Pittington to Sherburn North signalbox on the Leamside line provided access to the branch until its complete closure.

Shincliffe station was for many years used by the Durham Rural District Council Highways Department, but has since been turned into a private dwelling.

From 1949 Durham County Council used the Elvet station building as an office for the motor taxation department. The buildings were knocked down in 1964 and a new office block erected on the site. Durham Magistrates Court and student accommodation now occupy part of the site.

Parts of the Durham & Sunderland Railway have been turned into cyclepaths, classified as Regional Cycle Network route 20 and National Cycle Network route 14. A public footpath and cycleway follows the trackbed from Hetton to Sherburn but bypasses the Pittington station site.

The exterior of Durham Elvet station. (Lens of Sutton)

K1 2-6-0 No 62059 took in Waterhouses station with the 'West Durham Rail Tour' on 31st August 1958. (Beamish Museum)

The Deerness Valley branch

The Deerness Valley Railway, also known as the Waterhouses branch, was empowered by an Act of Parliament of 30th July 1855, and was sold to the North Eastern Railway on 13th July 1857. The railway ran from Deerness Valley Junction on the Durham to Bishop Auckland line to a point near the junction of the Stanley incline and the line to East Hedley Hope Colliery and was primarily built also to serve the Ushaw Moor, Waterhouses, Hamsteels, Esh, Cornsay and New Brancepeth collieries.

It opened for freight on 1st January 1858, but it was not for another two decades that passenger trains were introduced, the first service running on 1st November 1877. However, as on many other lines in the Durham coalfield, passenger trains were always a poor second in terms of revenue.

A basic terminus with a single platform terminus was built at Esh Winning, with the station being named Waterhouses. Although the line continued beyond Waterhouses for mineral traffic, passenger trains never used it. A second station was opened at Ushaw Moor on 1st September 1884.

The branch closed to passengers on 29th October 1951 and to freight on 28th December 1964. The terminus has long been demolished and the Deerness Valley Railway Path runs over much of the trackbed.

7

Steel from Consett

The Stanhope & Tyne Railway
The Lanchester line
The Derwent Valley line
The great ore line to Tyne Dock

In 1841 Consett was a village on the banks of the River Derwent with just 145 inhabitants. Today the population is more than 27,000. In between, it became County Durham's boom town. Beneath the wild and untamed rugged moors lay a vast wealth of riches. Firstly, there was blackband iron ore. Next, there were seams of coal that was particularly suited to coking. Around Consett there were plentiful supplies of limestone. These three ingredients were all that was needed for blast furnaces to turn out huge quantities of iron and steel.

Consett's origins lay in mining of a different sort, that of lead. Immigrant German cutlers and sword makers from Solingen who settled in the village of Shotley Bridge, now part of Consett, in the 17th century founded the steel industry here – and established it as the original home of Wilkinson Sword. For around 200 years the Derwent Valley was the centre of the British steel industry, because coal from Tyneside was readily available.

Heavy industry runs hand in hand with railways, and Consett found itself at the centre of a hub of lines, all of which are now closed.

For decades, the town was known for the cloud of red dust, airborne iron oxide from the steelmaking plant, that hung over it. Following the invention of Henry Bessemer's converter in 1855, steel could be made from British iron ore, which was otherwise too heavily contaminated by phosphorus. The converter eliminated the advantage of the blackband ores of the

Derwent Valley, and the emphasis of the British steel industry shifted to Sheffield.

The Stanhope & Tyne Railway

The village of Stanhope in the Wear Valley had two railways. In the valley, there was what is now the Weardale Railway, while an earlier line from South Shields and Consett approached from the north-east, before dropping down the side of the valley on two inclines. However, it served only large limestone quarries on the northern slopes of the valley, rather than Stanhope itself.

The moorland in the west of the Durham coalfield rises to a ridge between 800–900 ft above sea level, on which the pitheads of some of the biggest collieries are situated. To avoid the expense of major engineering works such as bridges, embankments and viaducts, rope haulage was widely used, allowing railways to be built more directly, often with extremely steep gradients, than would have been possible with horse or steam locomotive adhesion working.

The Stanhope & Tyne Railway, using a combination of rope-worked inclines and adhesion-operated stretches, with a summit at Parkhead 1,474 ft above sea level, was in many ways both challenging and revolutionary in its day. Apart from Snowdon, Parkhead was the highest railway summit in England and Wales, lying only 10 ft below the better-known London, Midland & Scottish Railway's Druimuachdar summit.

In 1831 a partnership was set up to acquire the leases of several collieries around Consett to secure rail access to the River Tyne. William Wallis of Westoe, now part of South Shields, agreed a lease with John Selby for coal seams under his property at West Consett. Wallis then formed a partnership with Cuthbert Rippon of Stanhope Castle and William Harrison of Monkwearmouth Grange for working coal at Medomsley and limestone at Stanhope. A railway was needed to link the two.

William Harrison looked at upgrading the existing Pontop Waggonway, but decided that the best solution would be to build a new railway from Stanhope to a point on the Tyne downriver from any bridges.

The partners avoided the expense of obtaining Parliamentary powers to build the railway by negotiating wayleaves, or permissions to cross private owners' lands. All of the landowners agreed, but the high charges imposed by some of the smaller ones, who were in effect holding the railway to ransom, did not pass without comment. However, most of the route ran over land owned by the Bishop and the Dean and Chapter of Durham who allowed right of way on reasonable terms. The Deed of Partnership for the Stanhope Railroad Company was prepared on 30th January 1832 and in April that year the partners leased both Pontop Colliery and the Stanhope limestone quarries.

The building of the railway began at Stanhope in early July 1832 with none other than Robert Stephenson taking on the role

The Crawleyside winding engine house near Stanhope on the Stanhope & Tyne Railway in the early 20th century. (Beamish Museum)

of consulting engineer and Thomas E. Harrison (William's son) as acting engineer.

A total of 14½ miles of the route between Stanhope and Annfield was worked by stationary winding engines and horses, and the other ¾ mile by gravity. The first locomotive arrived in South Shields on 1st May 1834.

The Stanhope–Annfield section was opened to traffic on 15th May that year. The terminus was situated near Lanehead Farmhouse ½ mile to the north of Stanhope, where limekilns were built at 796 ft above sea level. Waggons were drawn up from this point by the Crawley incline to the Crawley winding engine at 1,123 ft above sea level, and then up the Weatherhill incline to a summit at Whiteleahead. The next 1½ mile section to Parkhead Wheelhouse was worked by horse traction. From Parkhead, waggons were lowered down a 1½-mile incline to the stationary engine at Meeting Slacks. From there, the waggons continued downhill for a further 1¼ miles to Waskerley.

The line continued north-east from Waskerley downhill to Nanny Mayor's Bank, a self-acting incline, which was nearly ⅔ mile long with gradients of 1-in-10/13. A self-acting incline is designed so that laden waggons as they descend pull up empty waggons by means of a rope passing round a wheel at the crest of the hill, a process made possible by the fact that the gradients are in favour of the load. Nanny Mayor's Bank, named after Mrs Mayor of Tween House Farm, over whose land the railway passed, could handle eight waggons each way and there was an alehouse alongside the line at the bottom of the incline.

Horses hauled waggons over the next 1¼ miles to Healyfield Bridge, and then rode in dandy carts – waggons to accommodate horses when they were not needed to pull the trains – by gravity for 2 miles to White Hall and Cold Rowley.

Then came Hownes Gill, a 800 ft wide by 160 ft deep valley at the 10-mile point from Stanhope. The obvious idea of a viaduct was rejected as being too costly, and so the engineers looked for a cheaper way across the obstacle. The solution was to lay 7 ft gauge tracks on each face of the ravine, with gradients of 1-in-2.5 on the western side and 1-in-3 on the eastern. A special cradle or truck was built for each track, with the back wheels larger than

Loaded and unloaded waggons passing on the Stanley incline. (Beamish Museum)

those in front, as is the case with cliff or funicular railways, in order to keep the platform level. The standard gauge waggons were run onto one of these cradles and were lowered to the bottom, where they were transferred to the other cradle to be hauled up the other side. Both cradles worked simultaneously, and a small stationary engine situated at the bottom provided the power to haul the ropes.

Having crossed Hownes Gill, the line ran around the edge of an iron works at Consett, and from there along the ridge near the collieries of Stanley and Annfield Plain. It passed over the Pontop ridge on inclines worked by a stationary engine at the summit.

The lower, or eastern, section of the Stanhope & Tyne Railway, which involved no major engineering works and cost much less to build, was officially opened on 10th September 1834. Every form of motive power then available, namely, horses and locomotives, stationary engines and self-acting inclines, was used over various sections.

The opening of the first railway to South Shields provoked widespread celebrations; church bells were rung, royal salutes fired, and bands of musicians paraded the streets.

After the shipment on board the *Sally* of the first consignment of coal, which had been carried in 100 waggons from the Medomsley collieries, every railway staff member was given a substantial dinner. The proprietors and guests, totalling 121, were given a dinner at the Golden Lion by the townsfolk. It is recorded that the entire day's festivities passed off without the slightest incident, and that 'not a single case required the interference of the police'.

The railway did not live up to its founders' high expectations. Only two dividends were ever declared, one for the year 1835, and the other for the year 1836, both at the rate of 5%, and paid out of borrowed money.

In 1835 the railway began to carry passengers, at first in coal waggons without payment, and then in open carriages attached to the coal trains. The conveyance of passengers led to legal disputes, with landowners demanding extra payments on the basis that the right of wayleave had been granted for the conveyance of minerals only. By the end of 1840 the company was bankrupt and as it was not incorporated its members were jointly liable for its debts. The company gave up making lime and closed the line from Stanhope to Carrhouse (near Consett). Finding himself facing personal bankruptcy, Robert Stephenson moved to sort out the company's difficulties.

The proprietors agreed to promote a new statutory company to take over the property and debts. The old company was dissolved on 5th February 1841, and agreed to transfer the eastern part of the railway to a new company called the Pontop & South Shields Railway Company, incorporated by Act of Parliament on 23rd May 1842, and which raised capital to pay the debts. Early in 1842 the Derwent Iron Company bought the remaining section between Stanhope and Consett, along with the Stanhope limestone quarries.

The Derwent Iron Company wanted to link this line to the Stockton & Darlington Railway, and drew up plans for a railway from Waskerley to meet the Stockton & Darlington at Crook. In

1843 it obtained wayleaves for this purpose. Following this move, it agreed with the Stockton & Darlington that the latter would lease both the new line under construction and also the old railway between Stanhope and Consett.

The Stockton & Darlington Railway took possession of the lines in January 1845. The line from Crook to Waskerley Junction, known as the Weardale Extension Railway, was opened on 16th May 1845. On 1st April 1846, a passenger service to Cold Rowley was started, with the trains reversing at Waskerley Junction before running over a section of the Stanhope & Tyne line.

The Pontop & South Shields Railway was taken over on 1st January 1847 by the York & Newcastle Railway, which in turn in July 1854 became part the North Eastern Railway. On 3rd September 1858 the Stockton & Darlington took over the Derwent lines, and itself was absorbed by the NER in 1863. Therefore, the entire length of the original Stanhope & Tyne line was once more under single ownership.

During the 18 years that the Stanhope section of the line was run by the Stockton & Darlington, many improvements were made, replacing all the inclines with deviations, apart from the pair at Stanhope, which remained in use until 1851.

On 4th July 1859 the Waskerley deviation, namely, a line from Burnhill Junction making a descent to Whitehall Junction, was opened, and allowed trains from the Crook direction to run straight to Cold Rowley (renamed Rowley on 1st July 1869) without reversing at Waskerley Junction. After this, the old line between Waskerley Junction and Whitehall Junction was abandoned.

The Hownes Gill cliff lift was replaced on 1st June 1858 with a spectacular viaduct. Designed by Sir Thomas Bouch, who also drew up the plans for the first Tay Bridge, and made from around three million white firebricks, the stunning 12-arch viaduct was 700 ft long and 150 ft high, and thankfully is still with us today. That year a new line was opened to avoid Nanny Mayor's incline, which closed on 4th July 1859.

When the Waskerley deviation line was brought into use, locomotives could run all the way to Consett, and so the

Parkhead was opened as a goods-only station but early Stockton & Darlington passenger tickets show a Parkhead–Bishop Auckland service. A train may have run on market days, but it is believed unlikely it lasted after 1862. Parkhead was officially known as Blanchland from 1st July 1923. It closed on 2nd August 1965 and has been reopened as a bed and breakfast establishment with a tearoom, serving the cycleway that runs on the old Stanhope & Tyne trackbed alongside. (Author)

Stockton & Darlington passenger service was extended there. A station was built at Burnhill to serve Waskerley village via a moorland footpath, while a spur line was built from a point near Hownes Gill Viaduct to link the Stockton & Darlington line to the Lanchester branch of the NER (see below) and passenger trains were diverted to Blackhill station at Blackhill on the western side of Consett.

Passengers were conveyed on the line from the Crawley incline above Stanhope to Crook from 1st September 1845, but at first no stations were provided beyond Tow Law. The passenger service was cut back from Crawley to Waskerley in October

The magnificent Hownes Gill Viaduct, which replaced an unusual Stanhope & Tyne Railway cliff lift. (Brian Sharpe)

Rowley station, first known as Cold Rowley, survives at Beamish Museum and regularly sees passenger trains on the NER demonstration line. Hudswell Clarke saddle tank No 1366 of 1919 Renishaw Ironworks No 6, on loan from the nearly Tanfield Railway, hauled a restored Great Eastern Railway royal saloon on 16th April 2010. (Author)

1845, reintroduced on 1st April 1846, but was cancelled again at the end of that year, this time permanently.

Passenger trains from Crook to Waskerley were withdrawn in 1859 when the Waskerley deviation ran through nearby Burnhill instead. The line north of Tow Law to Blackhill was closed to passengers in May 1939. Weatherhill became the terminus of the old route to Stanhope after the above mentioned two inclines closed in 1951, and because of the fall off in stone traffic, the route closed from 1st May 1969.

Rowley station still has regular steam trains. In 1972 the main building was dismantled stone by stone and re-erected at Beamish Museum, where a short NER demonstration line complete with goods yard, signalbox and appropriate passenger and freight stock has been recreated. The station has been refurbished to its 1913 condition.

The Lanchester branch

An ironworks was first established at Consett in 1841. By 1860 Consett was taking off big time as a major ironmaking centre, and needed better access to the iron town of Middlesbrough and the neighbouring ironstone of the Cleveland Hills than the old

LNER K1 2-6-0 No 62059 calls at Lanchester with the 31st August 1958 'West Durham Rail Tour'. One member of is class survived into preservation, No 62005, which is based at the North Yorkshire Moors Railway and also operates on the main line. (Beamish Museum/Gordon Clarke)

Knitsley station on the Lanchester branch today, with the cyclepath running over the former trackbed. (Brian Sharpe)

Stanhope & Tyne route with its inclines, or the winding Stockton & Darlington line through Crook and Bishop Auckland, could offer. A direct route was required, so the NER built the Lanchester branch from Relly Mill Junction, south of Durham through the Browney valley to join the Stockton & Darlington south-west of Consett.

Building began in February 1861 and the branch officially opened on 1st September 1862. At first it was a single track line with stations at Consett, Knitsley, Lanchester and Witton Gilbert, and another later at Aldin Grange, later Bearpark, in 1883. Collieries sprung up at Bearpark, Malton, Lanchester and Langley Park. The biggest engineering feature was a 700 ft long, 70 ft high wooden viaduct crossing Knitsley Burn to the east of Knitsley. It is still there today but cannot be seen, because in 1915 when it needed major repairs, it was turned into an embankment using colliery slag and spoil. There were also several substantial stone bridges across the River Browney.

Passenger loadings on the 12-mile branch were always very light. The first casualty was Knitsley (which closed on 1st February 1916 but was reopened on 30th March 1925), and services were withdrawn as early as 1939. The stations were used once a year by Miners' Gala excursion trains until the last on 17th September 1954.

Freight continued until 5th July 1965 when Lanchester station became the last on the line to lose its goods facilities. The branch closed entirely on 20th June 1966 when mineral traffic was diverted to road transport, and Consett steelworks rail traffic was rerouted via Annfield Plain and South Pelaw.

The track was lifted in 1967, and much of the trackbed has been converted into the Lanchester Valley railway path and cycleway running from Lydgetts Junction just south of Consett to Broompark picnic area near Stonebridge.

The Derwent Valley line

The next railway to be opened to the ironmaking mecca of Consett was the Derwent Valley line on 2nd December 1867, built by the North Eastern Railway. Leaving the Newcastle & Carlisle Railway at Scotswood, it ascended through Rowlands Gill, where there was a deep 900-yard cutting, and Lintz Green to reach Blackhill. The four viaducts on the line included the 500 ft long Nine Arches Viaduct, which had to be built because the Earl of Strathmore refused to let the railway run over his Gibside Estate.

From the south, the intermediate stations were at Shotley Bridge, Ebchester, Lintz Green, Rowlands Gill and Swalwell, with High Westwood being opened in 1909.

Blackhill, where the livestock market was served by the station, went through several changes of identity. On the railway's blueprint it was Blackhill, but a change of mind led to its opening as Benfieldside. The name was changed to Consett in 1882. Benfieldside and Consett were next door to each other, but Consett was by now better known because of its industry. Three years later, the station became Consett & Blackhill. It finally

NER class O (LNER G5) 0-4-4 tank engine No 2084 pulling into Swalwell station. (Beamish Museum)

became Blackhill in 1896, to differentiate it from a new Consett station on the line to Annfield Plain and Birtley. The route was single track between Blackhill, where it made an end-on junction with the Lanchester Valley line at Lydgetts Junction, and Lintz Green, and double track between Lintz Green and Derwenthaugh at the northern end.

The passenger service evolved into a Newcastle–Blackhill–Lanchester–Durham operation – not bad for an area that, four decades before, had been so sparsely populated that it didn't warrant any passenger timetable.

Lintz Green station was the scene of an unsolved murder, when an unidentified gunman shot the stationmaster, Joseph Wilson, aged 60, on the night of Saturday, 7th October 1911. Wilson was on duty with booking clerk Fred White and porter John Routledge. The last train was late, a regular occurrence on a Saturday night, when the NER ran extra services taking late-night revellers home from Newcastle's pubs to the surrounding

The bridge over the River Derwent at Swalwell. (Brian Sharpe)

mining districts. After the train arrived at 10.42 pm, Wilson handed the driver the token for the single track section just to the west of the station, crossed the line under the bridge and entered the booking office. White extinguished the platform lamps, crossed the lines and joined Wilson in the booking office. Wilson wished him good night, left the office and walked 50 yards to his house.

White suddenly heard a shot, and joined by his friend Charles Swinburne, one of the four passengers who had got off at the station, ran out in the darkness to the stationmaster's house, to be met by Wilson's daughter Bertha who said her father had been shot. Despite efforts at first aid, Wilson died. A subsequent police investigation ascertained that he was killed by a single bullet from a large calibre revolver. The police found the bullet nearby, along with footprints in the garden, a linen cloth shaped to make a gag, and a small bag containing sand. The motive appeared to be robbery.

An inquest was opened in the first class waiting room on the Monday morning, a room decorated with certificates awarded to Wilson as winner of the NER Best Kept Station award for several years. At his funeral on the Tuesday, the stationmasters of Rowlands Gill, Scotswood, Ebchester and Shotley Bridge acted as pallbearers, while hundreds of local people followed the cortège to the cemetery at Leazes, three miles away.

More than 200 police officers were involved in the biggest manhunt in the region for many years. On the Wednesday, suspicion fell on Samuel Atkinson, 25, the station's relief porter, and he was arrested after police broke into his house. Three out of four witnesses picked him out as having been seen hanging round the station long after he told police he had gone home. Accordingly, he was charged with murder and hauled before Consett Police Court. Although it was pointed out that, prior to questioning, Atkinson had not been cautioned, and therefore any statement made by him as to his whereabouts on the evening in question must be inadmissible, he was eventually remanded in custody to Durham Assizes on 9th November. Yet after Atkinson was brought into the dock, to everyone's shock and surprise the local chief constable offered no evidence against the defendant and asked for him be discharged. The case was dismissed, but Atkinson's solicitors' request for expenses in preparing his case was refused, and the question of Atkinson's guilt or innocence has never been resolved.

Locals today talk in hushed whispers of the ghost of a tall man with a lantern, which haunts the old station.

At its peak before the First World War, the Derwent Valley route carried more than half a million passengers a year, while freight comprised iron ore to Consett and timber, bricks and coal to Newcastle. However, after the conflict ended, passengers began to use the more convenient buses instead, and by the forties, freight too was in decline.

Station closures began with High Westwood in 1942. Shotley Bridge and Ebchester closed in September 1953, Swalwell and Lintz Green in December 1953, Rowlands Gill in February 1954 and Blackhill on 23rd May 1955, when K1 class 2-6-0 No 62025

K1 2-6-0 No 62059 is seen at Rowlands Gill station on the Derwent Valley line hauling the 'West Durham Rail Tour' enthusiasts' special on 31st August 1958. (Beamish Museum)

hauled the final passenger train. Lorry traffic finally drove the last nail into the coffin of the freight services and the line closed altogether on 11th November 1963, the track being lifted the following year.

Durham County Council has turned the trackbed into a country park and cycleway, with the viaducts and bridges repaired. At Lydgetts Junction near Consett, the Derwent Valley route links with the C2C (Sea to Sea) Cycle Route, which includes Sustrans Consett–Sunderland cyclepath and the Waskerley Way, as well as the Lanchester Valley Railway Path.

The great ore line to Tyne Dock

By 1851 the ironstone deposits that had sparked off the sudden development of Consett as an iron and steel making centre were exhausted and it was necessary to import supplies of iron ore from the Cleveland Hills. Two decades later the Cleveland veins, which were the mainstay of the steel industry in Middlesbrough, were also drying up, so the producers turned to Bilbao for Spanish ore.

Consett still had rich supplies of local coal, so the steelworks continued to flourish. Ore was brought in from Sunderland Docks, and then Tyne Dock at South Shields.

Iron ore was first imported through Tyne Dock and carried over the Stanhope & Tyne route with its rope-worked inclines in 1880. A deviation line between East Castles and Annfield Plain was opened on 1st January 1886, eliminating the Pontop ridge inclines. However, it was not until another deviation, the North Eastern Railway route between Annfield and South Pelaw via Beamish, was opened in late 1893, that an incline-free route from Tyne Dock finally became available for the ore. This provided a

Tyne Dock coaling staithes in 1900. (Beamish Museum)

This 0-6-0 Kitson pannier tank was built in 1883 to the Stephenson 'long boiler' design for the Consett Iron & Steel Company where it worked on the intensive internal system. It ended its working life at Derwenthaugh Coke Works. It is now a static exhibit at the North Tyneside Steam Railway in Newcastle. (Paul Jarman/Beamish Musuem)

passenger service for the first time on this route, which was 22½ miles from Tyne Dock.

As elsewhere, the bus and motor car made it increasingly difficult for passenger services to break even, and the Consett to Newcastle via Annfield Plain trains were withdrawn during May 1955. The line remained open for freight, serving the steelworks and local collieries. Imports included iron ore, coke, coal and fuel oil, with steel products being exported. In February 1954 British Railways and the Consett Iron Co Ltd signed a 20-year contract for the movement of iron ore from Tyne Dock to Consett.

Local freight dropped to the point that by August 1964 the only station still left open for goods traffic was Consett.

The route is best remembered by enthusiasts for the sight of British Railways Standard 9F 2-10-0s hauling ore trains. Before

British Railways 9F 2-10-0 No 92062 passes beneath the footbridge at Beamish station (not to be confused with the nearby museum) with a tanker train. The Consett–Tyne Dock line was famous for its use of these very powerful locomotives. (Beamish Museum)

these magnificent machines, arguably the finest locomotives built by British Railways, NER T class 0-8-0s had been the mainstay of motive power until the turn of the century. The T3 sub class was introduced in 1919, when five appeared, followed by ten more in 1924. Later designated Q7s, they had three cylinders and produced 36,965 lbs of tractive effort, while a fleet of around four hundred 21-ton unbraked hopper waggons were used to carry the iron ore, being loaded at Tyne Dock by mechanical grabs and buckets.

The 1950s saw the introduction of automated loading and unloading of the 1¼ million tons of ore handled each year on the route. Thirty new bogie waggons were built at Shildon waggon works and introduced in late 1953, finally superseding the old waggons in February 1954. The new waggons had air-operated

One of the Q7 0-8-0s that made the Consett to Tyne Dock ore trains their own for so long, pictured at Consett in 1960. The Co-operative Society shop in the distance has since been re-erected at Beamish Museum. (Beamish Museum)

doors, which facilitated their speedy unloading at Consett, while the locomotives on the ore run had to be equipped with air pumps.

Ten dedicated 9Fs allocated to the route were fitted with Westinghouse air pumps before replacing the Q7 0-8-0s. The trains that they hauled were normally composed of eight or nine ore waggons and a brake van, the total weight being around 500 tons.

The final steam locomotive to be built by British Railways was a 9F No 92220, *Evening Star*, at Swindon in 1960. Rampant dieselisation in the 1960s saw the class finally replaced in November 1966 by ten class 24 BR/Sulzer Type 2 diesels based at Gateshead, which had additional air compressors/reservoirs and pipework fitted.

A definitive hive of heavy Durham industry now wiped off the face of the earth: Consett steelworks in 1958, as seen from the top of the gas holder. (Beamish Museum)

Consett steelworks provided jobs for 6,000 workers at its peak in the 1960s. However, by the time diesels took over the route, the writing was on the wall for the works. In fact, there are those who remain surprised that it had lasted so long. Following the working out of the ironstone deposits, the Durham coal seams began to become exhausted. The coal strata slopes from west to east, which means that the further east you dig, the deeper below ground the shafts must be sunk. Furthermore, the limestone quarries along the Stanhope & Tyne route began to become exhausted too. An alternative source was Weardale, with limestone brought in the roundabout way via Bishop Auckland and Lanchester.

In the 1970s, intense competition both from competitors on Teesside and from abroad led to much discussion about the future of the plant. The final years of Consett steelworks saw Swedish iron ore brought in from Teesside. Production of steel

This was the site of Consett station. Much of the surrounding trackbeds have been incorporated into road improvements. (Brian Sharpe)

Its design gives the impression that it harks back to the railway age, but this very modern structure in Stanley carries a cycleway alomg the former Consett–Tyne Dock route. (Author)

ended on 5th September 1980, and the works shut down completely a week later, with the loss of 3,700 jobs. It was a devastating blow to the town, where the unemployment rate was double the national average, at 15%, Consett soon becoming one of the worst unemployment blackspots in Britain.

The line through Annfield remained operational for another four years, while the once-proud steelworks was demolished and its remains transported away, leaving a gaping hole in the heart of the town.

Organised by the Derwentside Rail Action Group, the final passenger train to Consett ran on 17th March 1984. It carried more than 300 enthusiasts from all over Britain on a round trip from Newcastle, headed by class 46 Peak diesel No 46084, which on its front carried the 92066 number plate in memory of one of the famous Tyne Dock 9Fs.

The former signalbox from Carr House East at Consett is preserved at Rowley station in the Beamish Museum. (Author)

As with many other lost railways of Durham, the famous freight route was landscaped to form Sustrans' 26-mile Consett & Sunderland Railway path, National Cycle Network route number 7. Meanwhile, the project to build the second Tyne Tunnel involves the infilling of Tyne Dock basin with 400,000 cubic metres of sediment dredged from the Tyne, reclaiming 13 acres.

8

The Clarence Railway and Its Forgotten Electrics

A major rival to the Stockton & Darlington Railway emerged in the form of the Clarence Railway. In 1818, when Darlington businessmen applied for an Act of Parliament to build the Stockton & Darlington Railway, there was great disappointment in Stockton. Supporters there wanted a direct line to the Durham coalfield rather than one that ran through Darlington. When they realised that they were not going to win the day, the Stockton contingent decided to build their own line, from Haverton Hill on the north bank of the Tees to join the Stockton & Darlington at Simpasture Junction, just west of Newton Aycliffe. The route, authorised by Parliament on 25th May 1828, cut six miles off the 17-mile journey via Darlington, and with costs cut, the net result was cheaper coal at Stockton.

In 1830 the Stockton & Darlington extended southwards to Middlesbrough on the opposite side of the Tees, sparking off fierce competition between the two lines, and helping enormously to make that town what it is today.

The rival line was named the Clarence Railway, after the Duke of Clarence, the Lord High Admiral, who later became William IV, and the company's first Act of Parliament was obtained under this title.

The Clarence Railway opened in 1833. It terminated at Samphire Batts to the east of Haverton Hill half a mile upstream, which it also served. Samphire Batts was renamed Port Clarence around the time of the opening. The following year the first cargo of coal was shipped from Port Clarence in the brig *Elizabeth of London*. Before the railway came, the shipping of coal was difficult due to the shallow waters around Stockton. The opening of both railways provided the stimulus for the growth of both Middlesbrough and Port Clarence downstream. They enabled colliery owners to load coal onto ships for transportation to destinations like London. However, there were still navigational difficulties as far as Port Clarence was concerned, and the Clarence Railway did not make enough money for the first three years.

A second Act (1829) had authorised an extension of the Clarence Railway northwards from Stillington Junction to Byers Green in order to expand the railway's catchment area in the coalfield, with a branch to the city of Durham, which ended up going no further west than Thrislington, two miles north of Ferryhill. From Thrislington, there was another branch heading eastwards towards Sherburn, but it too fell short of its target, running only as far as Coxhoe, which it reached in 1837, although construction of the remainder of the proposed line had begun.

Between Ferryhill and Thrislington, the Clarence Railway chose a very convenient route through a break in the hills known as the Ferryhill Gap and carried out earthworks so that it could adapt it to build a railway on the level, a huge advantage. The same route through the gap was later followed by the Newcastle & Darlington Junction Railway, which is now part of the East Coast Main Line.

The Clarence Railway's so-called Durham branch from Stillington Junction to Thrislington, and the 'Sherburn' branch to Coxhoe opened for freight on 16th January 1834, and to passengers on 11th July 1835. The carriages were pulled by horses and a connecting horse bus took the passengers on to Durham.

The 'main' branch to Byers Green saw horse-drawn coal traffic introduced on 31st March 1837, four years before the line was completed. At Byers Green, there was an end-on junction with the West Durham Railway, which opened in 1840. From Byers Green, the West Durham ran to Todd Hill and then down an incline to the River Wear before running up Sunnybrow incline to Helmington, skirting the northern side of Crook and reaching Whitelee Colliery in 1841.

Jumping ahead here, by way of explanation to make sense of

a complicated network of railways, which was improved by the elimination of inclined planes by circuitous detours, in 1867 a deviation line around Sunniside incline to the west of Whitelee joined the West Durham Railway at West Durham Junction, and in 1885 the NER line from Bishop Auckland joined the Clarence Railway route at Burnhouse Junction.

Just as the Clarence Railway had annoyed the Stockton & Darlington by being built, the former was to face a battle with a new competitor in the east, the Great North of England, Clarence & Hartlepool Junction Railway (GNECHJR), which aimed to carry coal from West Durham to Hartlepool, avoiding both Port Clarence and the longer Stockton to Hartlepool lines. The GNECHJR set out to link all three lines in its title, but it never managed to reach the original Great North of England Railway until its successor had extended the line north of Darlington to Newcastle.

The blueprint for the GNECHJR was a route running westwards from the Hartlepool Dock & Railway Company's Wingate Colliery branch, eight miles to Thrislington, where there would be a connection with the Clarence Railway's Byers Green branch and also the then-still-planned Great North of England Railway. Clarence directors immediately recognised the threat posed by the GNECHJR, producing a route to the port of Hartlepool that was eight miles shorter than the existing line to Port Clarence. Recalling what it had done to the S&DR, the Clarence was to be given a taste of its own medicine!

Panicking, the Clarence board began to do everything it could to stop the GNECHJR in its tracks, or rather, before they were laid. There were several court battles, and a confrontation at Thrislington, where a crossing of the Clarence Railway's 'Sherburn' branch on the level at no less than three points was planned, all of which conspired to hold up the construction of GNECHJR for seven years.

When the GNECHJR reached Thrislington from the east on 11th July 1839, the Clarence Railway decided to take matters into its own hands, or rather, that of its workmen. The GNECHJR laid one of the crossings, only for it to be ripped up straightaway by Clarence permanent way staff. The Clarence then obtained a court injunction in 1841 to stop further incursions by the GNECHJR, which loudly protested that it was tantamount to unfair competition.

The matter was finally settled by an Act of Parliament of 28th July 1843, which allowed the GNECHJR to cross the Clarence on a bridge over the 'Sherburn' branch and another over the former Great North of England route, which was built in the end by the Newcastle & Darlington Railway. Of course, in reality, the Clarence had not been as bothered about the crossings, inconvenient as three would be, as about the wholesale loss of trade to Hartlepool.

Work on the bridge over the Clarence line began in December 1843, but to their horror a fortnight later the GNECHJR directors were told that the works were being 'interfered with' by several men believed to be acting on behalf of the Clarence. The GNECHJR applied to a local magistrate to bind over both sides to keep the peace, but he declined to make any such order. This particular battle was won by the GNECHJR only when it bought extra land on which to build the bridge piers as opposed to constructing on Clarence territory.

The next Clarence spoiling tactic was to spread the word amongst colliery owners that the GNECHJR had no powers to cross the 'Sherburn' branch and would never provide the promised fast coal route to Hartlepool, and offered them the chance to sign long-term contracts binding them to the Port Clarence route. The enraged GNECHJR quickly issued a statement in rebuttal.

Following this, the Clarence built two walls on its land, impeding the construction of the GNECHJR bridge, with the rival company pointing out this was in breach of its empowering Act.

The Newcastle & Darlington Junction Railway arrived in 1844 and crossed the Clarence's Byers Green line at the north end of the Ferryhill Gap. The crossing was abolished in 1873 following an accident.

In 1845 the GNECHJR obtained powers to build a short curving branch to link its line at Thrislington to the Newcastle & Darlington Junction Railway at what became Thinford Junction. After that the Clarence opposition to the crossing lessened somewhat, as the damage was by then done by the provision of another route to the coalfield it could do little about. However, in August that year the GNECHJR saw fit to obtain another injunction to prevent damage to its bridge works over the Clarence.

The Hartlepool Dock & Railway had been set up by Clarence Railway founder Christopher Tennant in 1831. Because of the navigational problems to Port Clarence, Tennant came up with the idea of extending the Clarence Railway eastwards to Hartlepool, where the harbour opened on 1st July 1835. In 1845 the Hartlepool Dock & Railway leased the GNECHJR, and in 1846 both lines were taken over by the York & Newcastle Railway. In 1848 the York, Newcastle & Berwick Railway took a lease on the GNECHJR for a period of 999 years. This move ended the disagreement over the junction at Thrislington, and so finally both the link to join the Byers Green branch and the curve to Thinford Junction were completed.

A passenger service between Hartlepool and Ferryhill began on 13th October 1846, with trains reversing at Thinford Junction to join the Newcastle & Darlington Junction line southwards to Ferryhill, as the curve from the Hartlepool line giving direct access to Ferryhill was not built until later. That November, freight first moved over the long-contentious bridge from the Byers Green branch to the GNECHJR.

In 1844 the Clarence Railway was leased to the Stockton & Hartlepool Railway, and was taken over by the West Hartlepool Harbour & Railway in 1853, while the following year the North Eastern Railway took over the lease on the GNECHJR. The West Hartlepool Harbour & Railway became part of the NER in 1865.

In 1871 a new link from Relly Mill Junction south of Durham to Hoggersgate Junction, north of Thinford Junction was opened. It became a section of today's East Coast Main line, relegating the Leamside line to secondary status. This link opened to freight in September 1871 and received its first express passenger trains on 15th January 1872, with stopping passenger trains following on 1st March that year.

The opening of the link saw a flying junction built at Coxhoe Junction near Thrislington, with the lines from Ferryhill to Byers

Green and Hartlepool ascending on the east side of the Newcastle & Darlington Junction main line. The Byers Green branch then crossed the Clarence's Coxhoe branch and the Newcastle & Darlington on a girder bridge, before rejoining the old Clarence route to the west, and the Hartlepool route picked up the original GNECHJR line. From then on it was possible for trains to run from Ferryhill to Hartlepool without reversing at Thinford Junction.

In 1870 the NER finally took over the West Durham Railway, which linked the Byers Green line to numerous collieries, and which had faced stiff competition from the Stockton & Darlington. Passenger trains between Ferryhill and Tod Hills were introduced, and the NER built a new station at the latter eight years after, along with a substantial locomotive shed. Because most of the mines could be served by other routes, an Act of 1891 allowed the NER to abandon most of the West Durham Railway east of the River Wear. The last section, that from Tod Hills to Burnhouse Junction, was used until the early 1930s.

Meanwhile, decades after the squabbling over its northern

Redmarshall station, formerly Carlton, served a key junction on the Clarence Railway. (Lens of Sutton)

Stillington station lay near the junction of the Clarence Railway main line and its northern branch leading to Ferryhill, Thrislington, Coxhoe and, most importantly, Byers Green. (Lens of Sutton)

branches, the Clarence Railway main line was poised to make railway history.

From 1882 onwards, the length between Stillington North Junction and Redmarshall (initially named Carlton) was widened to four tracks. At Redmarshall, two lines turned off to Carlton South Junction and the Wellfield to Bowesfield Junction line. This enabled passenger services from the Ferryhill direction to Teesside to run through Stillington North Junction at the same time as a freight train from Shildon to Newport Yard.

In 1910 Vincent Raven was appointed by the NER as the chief mechanical engineer and, ahead of his time, looked at introducing electric locomotives to the main line – 55 years before the British Railways Modernisation Plan. In 1913 he was given permission to use the 18-mile route from Shildon Yard, a collection point for coal, to Newport Yard, a distribution point for coal to docks, blast furnaces, and iron works in the Stockton-Newport area, as a testbed prior to electrifying the busy York to

Newcastle main line. Electrification using a 1,500V DC overhead system began the following year, with the first stage being opened on 1st July 1915, and the entire scheme completed on 10th January 1916.

Ten 0-4+4-0 freight locomotives designed by Raven and numbered 3 to 12 were built by Darlington Works between 1914 and 1919, with electrical equipment supplied by Siemens Bros, including twin pantographs on the central cab roof to pick up the overhead supply. They were designed to start a 1,400-ton train and haul it on the level at a minimum speed of 25 mph. They ran well, and were thought to be better than the NER's T2 0-8-0 freight engines, giving a foretaste of the eventual end of steam. Indeed, Shildon's No 3 steam roundhouse was converted to accommodate all ten electric locomotives.

However, a downturn in the coal traffic on the line meant that there was never enough work for the ten to do. Following the restrictions on coal movements in the First World War, the coal

The first of the Clarence Railway route's pioneering electric freight locomotives in North Eastern Railway livery. It began trials along the route in 1915. (Beamish Museum)

trade continued to be depressed in the 1920s and 1930s, by which time the overhead system needed replacing. At this point the mineral traffic had dropped to the point where it was considered not worth spending the money, so it was decided to take down the wires and masts and revert to steam. The equipment was dismantled between 7th January and 8th July 1935, and the locomotives placed into storage.

The LNER planned to electrify the Manchester–Sheffield–Wath line (the Woodhead Route) as early as the 1930s, but the Second World War got in the way and it did not happen until 1954, six years after nationalisation. The LNER looked at converting the Shildon locomotives into banking engines for this route, and one of them, No 11, was duly modified at Doncaster Works, but was not even tested. In October 1945 all ten were designated class EB1 (Electric Banking 1), even though only one had been turned into a banking engine, After nationalisation, they were renumbered as 26502-11.

In 1949 EB1 No 26510 was transferred to Ilford for shunting duties at the new electric carriage sheds built for the London Liverpool Street to Shenfield electrification. However, there was no further use for the others, which were broken up in 1950–51. No 26510 was renumbered Departmental No 100 in January 1959, and made its final run on 4th November 1960 when the Shenfield line in Essex was converted to AC operation. As a 'one off', No 100 was not converted to AC operation, and was officially withdrawn in April 1964. Sadly, it was not preserved – the heritage railway movement was very much in its infancy at that stage and all the emphasis was on saving classic steam types from extinction – and so a unique piece of Durham transport history was lost forever.

Apart from a brief period in 1841/2, the Shildon–Newport line never saw timetabled passenger trains, although it was used in the summer for holiday traffic from Bishop Auckland and Shildon to the local seaside resorts of Seaton Carew, Redcar and Saltburn. However, it came into its own during the Second World War, when passenger services were laid on for the workers at the Royal Ordnance Factory at Aycliffe, where two new stations were specially provided in January 1942 at Demons

Bridge and East Simpasture on a branch from the Clarence line. At Demons Bridge, the new station had six platforms to cope with the special trains carrying workers, while Simpasture East had four platforms to cope with similar services from the north-west.

After the government demanded an urgent increase in munitions production for the army, work began in May 1940 to construct the huge munitions factory, which employed some 17,000 workers, nearly 90% of them women, between 1941 and 1945. It was primarily a filling and assembly plant, putting powder into shells and bullets, assembling detonators and fuses, with ammunition casings made at another Royal Ordnance Factory at Spennymoor. Needless to say, the work was highly dangerous, and in one of several explosions, eight women were killed.

Nevertheless, some workers lied about their age to join the war effort there. One worker said she was 49, yet was later found out to be 69. She was decorated by King George VI for her work. On 15th May 1942, Winston Churchill visited the factory to boost morale.

In 1945 the plant became redundant, with the special trains ending, and the following year, work began on converting the site into the Aycliffe Industrial Estate, this industrial development being the beginning of today's Newton Aycliffe. In 1947 Aycliffe was designated as a new town for post-war development and Durham County Police opened its headquarters in some of the redundant buildings. Like so many cities and towns in Britain today, it owes its development to its place on the railway network.

The section of the route between Simpasture Junction on the Stockton & Darlington line south of Bishop Auckland to Teesside's Stillington North Junction closed in June 1943. However, although the trackbed is overgrown, some of the bases of the masts used for the electric wires can be located.

The passenger service over the former main line of the Clarence Railway from Stockton via Redmarshall, Stillington, and Sedgefield, was withdrawn from 31st March 1952.

The final passenger train between Ferryhill and West

All that remains of Byers Green station, where the Clarence and West Durham railways met. The trackbed is now part of the Auckland Way cyclepath. (Oliver Green/Creative Commons)

Hartlepool ran on 7th July 1952, but much of the line lingered on for mineral traffic until 1965.

As for the initial part of the Clarence Railway, passenger services from Haverton Hill, which grew up with the development for a major salt industry in the late 19th century, to Port Clarence were withdrawn as early as 1939, despite the fact that in 1925 there had been fourteen trains in each direction with six more on Saturdays. Services from Billingham to Haverton Hill, which included the intermediate station of Belasis Lane (opened 1929), ended on 14th June 1944. Unadvertised workmen's services on the short line soldiered on until 6th

Seen better days, but still standing: the signalbox at Port Clarence. (Mick Garratt/Creative Commons)

November 1961. This branch remained open for freight, and indeed, between 1971 and 1977, an extension to Seal Sands was built to serve a petro-chemical storage plant. It was last 'reclaimed' by a steam-hauled passenger train on 10th May 2008 when LNER K1 2-6-0 No 62005 *Lord of the Isles* and class 47 diesel No 47760 ran the 'The East Coast Explorer' from Newcastle upon Tyne via several locations including Port Clarence, the site of the northern end of the Middlesbrough Transporter Bridge, and Seal Sands.

On the subject of the long-gone passenger services on the Port Clarence line, and pioneering forms of modern traction, mention must be made of the NER's early experimentation with petrol-electric railcars here. In 1903 a pair similar in design to the Tyneside electric stock of the same period was built, with electric motors driving the axles of the power bogie via gears. Reversible seats on both sides of a central gangway provided seating for 52 passengers and interior electric lighting was provided. In a world where steam's dominance on the main line was unchallenged, they were revolutionary.

Numbered 3170 and 3171, they entered service in August 1904. Intended for the short trip between Hartlepool and West Hartlepool, at least one of them ran between Billingham and Port Clarence in December 1904. However, they were not considered a success, and were replaced by steam on this route a month later. The railcars afterwards worked on the NER's Scarborough–Filey service, the Cawood branch near Selby and services out of Ripon.

The railcars were withdrawn between 31st May and 4th April 1931. The body of No 3170 was sold to a North Yorkshire landowner and survived for several decades as a holiday home. After falling derelict, it was 'rediscovered' by award-winning coach restorer Stephen Middleton, who founded the 1903 Electric Autocar Trust to restore it to running order at the Embsay & Bolton Abbey Steam Railway in West Yorkshire, albeit with a modern diesel engine. Parts have been located, along with a suitable trailer car. The net result may not be another *Flying Scotsman*, but will be a re-creation of a hugely-important missing link in Britain's railway history. Most of Britain's passenger trains today comprise diesel or electric multiple units, as opposed to locomotive-hauled services, and anyone tracing their evolution will find No 3170 an excellent place to start.

9

Stockton to Sunderland and the Castle Eden Line

A direct route between Stockton and Sunderland also passed into the pages of history. It was in 1835 that the Hartlepool Dock & Railway extended northwards to Haswell, leaving the existing Hartlepool–Sunderland route at Hart before climbing Hesleden Bank to Hesleden (opened 1891), Castle Eden (1839), Thornley (1858), Shotton Bridge (1864) and finally Haswell. There, its first terminus was not only at right angles to that of the Durham & Sunderland Railway, which reached Haswell from the north the following year, but was on a different level from it. A station at

Bowesfield Junction, the southern end of the Stockton & Castle Eden branch in the early 1950s. (J.W. Armstrong Trust Collection)

Wellfield was added in 1882 and superseded Thornley in providing connections between Hartlepool–Sunderland and Stockton trains.

The Hartlepool company began building an extension from Haswell to Moorsley to join the Durham Junction Railway but abandoned the scheme. The Hartlepool line and the Durham & Sunderland were joined at Haswell and through running became possible with a new station opening in 1877. As an aside, Haswell was the site of the world's first coal mine with a steel cable down its mine shaft, an innovation that revolutionised the coal mining industry, just as steam locomotive development in County Durham changed global transport technology forever.

In 1880 the northern section of the North Eastern Railway's Stockton & Castle Eden branch joined the Hartlepool–Haswell–Sunderland route. Known locally as the 'Cuckoo Line', this route ran northwards from Bowesfield Junction at Stockton to Wellfield, the first section being opened to freight

Shotton Colliery was served by a mineral line linking it to the main line at Shotton Bridge between Haswell and Thornley. It is also the name of the village that sprang up around the mine where the shaft was sunk in 1840. In 1972 the National Coal Board announced that the mine would close, with the loss of 800 jobs. The local brickworks and coke works went with the pit and there is almost no work in the village today. (Beamish Museum)

on 1st May 1877, providing access to the coalfields of south Durham.

The first passenger services over part of the Stockton & Castle Eden line started on 1st March 1880 and ran throughout from Stockton to Wellfield on 1st May 1889.

Despite the route's name, it did not physically serve Castle Eden, which was renowned for its now demolished Castle Eden Brewery and Castle Eden Ale. Services ran between Stockton and Wellfield, which were provided for the mining village of Wingate, and there passengers could change for the Hartlepool Dock & Railway line and travel eastwards to Castle Eden, the next station.

The line's creation was brought about by the continuing

expansion of industry both in the Durham coalfield and Teesside, which in late Victorian times was one of the fastest-growing industrial centres in the world, largely thanks to its excellent rail and sea connections, which provided the vital mineral resources.

Despite the fact that several rival schemes had by the 1870s been brought together under the banner of the North Eastern Railway, some routes were becoming congested, and the centres of coalmining in the north of the county were slowly moving as older pits became exhausted and needed to be replaced.

The promoters of the Stockton & Castle Eden branch had the primary aims of bypassing both Hartlepool and Stockton, and joining the Hartlepool–Sunderland and Middlesbrough–Darlington lines.

The principal contractor for the 'Cuckoo Line' was Thomas Nelson, a well-known railway builder, who started it in 1875. The main structure required was a 22-arch viaduct at Thorpe Thewles across the Thorpe Beck Valley. Using eight million bricks, it cost £37,000.

The mineral traffic primarily comprised Durham coal, Weardale limestone, and Cleveland ironstone to support the mushrooming industries on Teesside, along with livestock and agricultural produce. However, the line travelled through a thinly-populated area, and passenger services very much came second in importance.

The intermediate station of Thorpe Thewles served Grindon, a place with a population of just 345, while Thorpe Thewles village itself was served by Carlton (later Redmarshall) station on the Clarence Railway, over which the Stockton & Castle Eden branch ran, and to which it was joined by a pair of connecting curves built in 1877/8. Again, this was a main objective for the promoters: the junction with the Clarence Railway between Port Clarence and Shildon and Ferryhill provided access to the industrial centres on the north bank of the Tees.

Further north, Wynyard and Hurworth Burn stations were used by just a few farmsteads. However, Wellfield served several mining communities and generated substantial passenger numbers for Stockton market days.

A pair of NER-built J27 0-6-0s on duty alongside Silkworth signalbox in British Railways days. The signalbox near Ryhope Junction on the Sunderland–Stockton line controlled the junction where the mineral lines to Ryhope and Silkworth collieries diverged. (Author's Collection)

When the Stockton & Castle Eden line opened, some of the more important through trains were diverted onto it, missing out West Hartlepool altogether.

Despite the comparative obscurity of this route, it was used by express trains from Newcastle to Manchester and Liverpool, and Oxford and Bournemouth, but they stopped only at Stockton and Sunderland. In 1894 permission was granted to Lord and Lady Londonderry of Wynyard Hall to stop the 7.30 am from Newcastle and the 6.30 pm from York at Thorpe Thewles station if required. It is said that when royalty arrived at Thorpe Thewles to visit the Londonderry family, a red carpet was rolled out, and the hedge along the roadside was specially cut and lit by oil lamps for the royal coach that would take the party on to Wynyard Hall.

As an express passenger route, the line was downgraded as

early as 1905 when today's coastal route between Sunderland and West Hartlepool was opened. Poorly patronised by passengers, in 1925 there were just four trains each way per day between Stockton and Wellfield, and eight between West Hartlepool and Sunderland.

The Stockton & Castle Eden branch lost its passenger services south of Wellfield as early as 2nd November 1931, and was closed as a through route on 6th July 1966 and the last section from Carlton Junction to Bowesfield Junction was axed in 1968. The West Hartlepool–Haswell–Sunderland service continued until 9th June 1952, while services on the Great North of England, Clarence & Hartlepool Junction Railway (see Chapter 8) between Hartlepool, Castle Eden and Ferryhill ended on 7th June 1952. The passenger service from Ferryhill originally terminated at Hartlepool, but with the expansion of West Hartlepool at the former's expense, the GNCHJR was diverted to West Hartlepool, with a shuttle service linking it to Hartlepool. This service was withdrawn from the public

Murton station, on the Durham & Sunderland Railway's section of the Sunderland–Stockton route via Wellfield. (Lens of Sutton)

Thorpe Thewles station survives as the visitor centre for Wynyard Woodland Park & Planetarium. (Wynyard Woodland Park)

timetable on 16th June 1947, but kept on for school pupils until 23rd March 1964.

The magnificent viaduct on the Stockton & Castle Eden branch was demolished in 1979 to make way for the Thorpe Thewles bypass. In 1977, Cleveland County Council bought the Cleveland end of the overgrown disused trackbed to develop a long-distance footpath with grant aid from the Department of the Environment and the Countryside Commission. It opened to the public in 1981. The old stationmaster's house at Thorpe Thewles was opened as a visitor centre in 1983. It now forms the centre of Wynyard Woodland Park & Planetarium.

10
The Great Private Freight Systems

Lambton, Hetton & Joicey
Bowes
Tanfield
Brandling Junction
South Hetton
Londonderry

While this book, like others in the series, is primarily concerned with passenger-carrying lines that formed part of the network inherited and then severely pruned by British Railways, the carriage of mineral traffic was, as we have seen, of paramount importance in Durham and Teesside. The public railways were just part of the story. Co-existing with the North Eastern Railway were numerous private lines, ranging in size from short horse-drawn waggonways to sprawling systems connecting many collieries to the wharves and coal staithes.

An analogy may be drawn with animal metabolism, which is based around a system of blood vessels. The body also contains a second set of conduits as part of the lymphatic system, which distributes the fluid known as lymph. Both systems perform different functions, yet operate alongside each other and in a similar manner. Some of the private Durham systems had little need to interact with the national rail network as far as their day-to-day business was concerned, and acted wholly independently of it, to the point of running their own private passenger trains for workers. Most, however, were adjuncts to the network, private lines often several miles long leading from the main line to a colliery or works. In some cases, such as the Lambton,

Hetton & Joicey Colliery, the distinction was blurred, with privately-owned locomotives and stock having the rare permission to run over parts of the national network.

Long before the steam engine arrived on the scene, a myriad of horse-drawn waggonways were tapping the vast mineral wealth on the south Durham coalfield. The steam engine facilitated expansion on an industrial scale, and though most of the region's railway routes, both public and private, are no longer with us, nonetheless they shaped the landscape that we have inherited today.

To cover every lost private railway in Durham and Teesside would be a task of encyclopaedic proportions, but here is a resumé of some of the bigger and more important operations.

Lambton, Hetton & Joicey

The Lambton railway system dates back nearly three centuries to the opening of a waggonway between Fatfield and Cox Green in 1737, with early steam locomotives introduced around 1814. In 1819 J.G. Lambton, who later became the Earl of Lambton, bought the Newbottle Waggonway, a 5¾-mile concern that linked mines to deep water berthing at Sunderland, and joined it to the Lambton Waggonway. A new line between Burnmoor and Philadelphia, near Houghton-le-Spring, afforded his coal waggons direct access to the River Wear at Sunderland. This new route was worked by stationary engines until the mid 1860s.

After the North Eastern Railway opened its branch from Penshaw on the Leamside line to Sunderland via Cox Green and Pallion in 1865, close to the Lambton network, and a branch from Pallion to Deptford Wharf on the Wear close to Lambton Staithes the same year, an agreement was drawn up between the NER and the Lambton Railway. It granted permission for Lambton Railway locomotives to run over the NER between Penshaw and Lambton Staithes and later to Sunderland South Dock, and a series of 0-6-0 locomotives was ordered for the purpose.

By Edwardian times, this fleet was becoming outdated for long-haul coal trains from the collieries to the coast, so the Lambton Railway looked to the successful 0-6-2 tank engines being used for heavy coal traffic in the South Wales valleys. In 1904 an 0-6-2T was bought from Kitson of Leeds and it became the railway's No 29; another six of the type followed, from different manufacturers, between then and 1934. They included No 5, built in 1909 by Robert Stephenson at Darlington. Both Nos 5 and 29 are now part of the North Yorkshire Moors Railway collection.

In 1911 the Lambton system took over the Hetton Railway (see Chapter 1) and built a tunnel bypassing the latter's series of rope inclines to give steam locomotives access to its northern reaches, including Hetton Staithes, for the first time.

The Lambton system was further expanded in 1924 with the addition of the Joicey colleries, forming the Lambton, Hetton & Joicey Colliery (LHJC). By the time it became part of the National Coal Board in 1947, it had 57 locomotives. More 0-6-2Ts were needed, and the LHJC looked to the Great Western

Preserved Lambton, Hetton & Joicey Railway No 29, heading a North Yorkshire Moors Railway passenger service. (Brian Sharpe)

Railway, which had inherited several smaller railways in South Wales in 1923 and soon afterwards declared most of their locomotives redundant as non-standard. Taff Vale Railway 0-6-2T No 85 was bought in 1929, and continued to work until 1968, when the NCB withdrew it. It is now part of the Keighley & Worth Valley Railway fleet.

The overhaul of all Lambton locomotives was undertaken at the line's Philadelphia engine works. Like the system it served, it was a sprawling affair that not only handled locomotive maintenance and waggon building and repairs, but also provided engineering facilities for local collieries and the company's shipping fleet.

With the decline of the Durham coalfield setting in, the Hetton Railway via Warden Law was closed in 1959, followed by Lambton Staithes in January 1967 and the line to Pallion in August that same year, ending hauling over the national network by the company's locomotives. Steam locomotive working on the system ended in February 1969. The final section of the Hetton Railway closed on 3rd June 1972, while Herrington Colliery, the last served by the system, closed on 20th November 1985. The final section of the LHJC system, between Lambton Coke works and Penshaw, closed in January 1986. Philadelphia works was closed piece by piece, and finally shut its doors on 22nd December 1989.

Three other LHJC locomotives survive in preservation: Hawthorn Leslie 0-4-0 saddle tank No 14, built in Newcastle in 1914 and now on the Tanfield Railway; Hunslet 0-6-0ST No 60, built in 1948 for the National Coal Board (Durham Area) and now on the Strathspey Railway at Aviemore; and a second Taff Vale 0-6-2T, No 28, sold by the GWR to the Longmoor Military Railway and acquired by the NCB in 1948. It is now part of the National Railway Museum's collection.

Bowes

In earlier chapters we have seen the frequent use of cable-hauled inclines on many of the pioneer railways of the Durham coalfield, not least the groundbreaking undertaking that was the Stanhope & Tyne Railway. Today, only one preserved but operational standard gauge cable-hauled incline exists in the world, on the sole surviving part of another of Durham's greatest industrial lines, the Bowes Railway.

The line was built by George Stephenson in 1826 to transport coal from the pits to the Tyne staithes. It was largely based on Stephenson's earlier Hetton Railway and initially served a new colliery at Springwell. Running to Black Fell, Jarrow, the first section had two inclined planes powered by stationary engines. The self-acting incline from Springwell Colliery down to Lingey Lane was still working in the 1960s. Locomotives were used from there to Jarrow.

The line took its name from the family of George Bowes, who inherited the Gibside estate which included some of County Durham's richest coal seams. Also serving as MP for Durham, in 1726 he became a founder of the Grand Alliance of coal owners, a cartel for the control of the London coal trade. His family would include Elizabeth Bowes-Lyon, better known as the late Queen Mother. It was his descendant John Bowes who in 1836 formed the Marley Hill Coal Company to reopen Marley Hill Colliery on the Gibside estate, and who rebuilt the line from Bowes Bridge and Marley Hill westwards to Burnopfield and Dipton.

The Bowes system, also known as the Pontop & Jarrow Railway, expanded in stages until 1855, with the opening of the final section from Burnopfield via Pickering Nook to Dipton Delight Colliery. Along with other colliery lines in County Durham, it was nationalised in 1947.

The Bowes Railway ran a passenger service between Jarrow and Springwell station at Wardley until 1872, but later issued permits to workmen to travel on the line to and from work, either behind a locomotive or even by waggon on the inclines.

In the mid 20th century the NCB fulfilled a long-mooted idea of linking the Bowes Railway to the Pelaw Main Railway, with a 100-yard link from the latter's Eighton Banks incline to the former's Blackham's Hill East incline. The Pelaw Main Railway, also known as the Ouston & Pelaw Waggonway, dated back to

Carrying NCB livery, 1949-built Barclay 0-4-0 saddle tank No 22, at work on today's Bowes Railway heritage line. The locomotive was built new for the Bowes Railway as No 22 and was later renumbered 85. It is the only original Bowes locomotive to survive, having been transferred to St Anthony's Tar Works in Newcastle in 1970, and withdrawn in 1973, before being preserved three years later. (Brian Sharpe)

N C. B.
AREA 'B' GROUP
No 22

1809 and used rope from the coal pits at Urpeth. A branch from pits in the Team Valley joined the railway at White Hill. There was a stationary hauling engine at Team Colliery where the waggonway passed under the A167 Durham road, with another in Wrekenton where Gateshead Electric Tramways crossed the waggonway until 1951. Locomotives were later used to haul coal up the steep inclines from Team Valley.

In January 1955 the two railways were amalgamated, with parts of the Pelaw Main closed as part of the rationalisation that immediately followed. The merger effectively added a 6½-mile branch to the Bowes and made the combined operation the biggest colliery railway system in County Durham. By the mid 1960s, it was the last of the great Durham colliery railways to still be operational.

It would not last, despite surveys that showed it was still cheaper to use the railway to carry coal than to send it by road.

The final section of the Pelaw Main Railway closed on 18th April 1873, with demolition of the buildings following soon afterwards. This left the Bowes Railway serving just Kibblesworth and Unsworth collieries. Their closure was announced in 1974, along with the railway's five remaining inclines. The last coal left Kibblesworth on 4th October 1974, a local TV camera recording the event for broadcasting the same day.

It would not be the end of the Bowes Railway, for that year Tyne & Wear Council looked at the possibility of preserving part of the redundant line, and chose the section between Black Fell Bank Head and Springwell Bank Head, including the waggon and engineering shops at Springwell and a huge fleet of different types of waggons. Today, the Bowes Railway is not only a heritage steam line but also a scheduled ancient monument. Based at Springwell Village, it has 1¼ miles of rope-hauled incline railway, and 1½ miles of the old Wrekenton extension of the Pelaw Main line for steam and diesel-hauled passenger trips. It includes Springwell Bank Foot shed, said to be the oldest loco shed in the world, and also boasts the biggest collection of colliery waggons in Britain. The railway is open for static viewing from Mondays to Saturdays, with steamings on selected dates.

One section of the old system to Jarrow survived the closure between Kibblesworth Colliery and Springwell Bank Foot, serving Monkton (formerly Wardley) Coal Treatment Plant. To differentiate it from the preservation scheme, the NCB renamed it Monkton Railways in 1975. The coal treatment plant closed on 19th July 1985 followed by Jarrow Staithes in December that year. Rail traffic finally ended on the last surviving stretch of commercial use, the mile between Monkton Coking Plant and British Railway's Leamside line at Wardley signalbox, on 10th January 1986, almost 160 years to the day that Stephenson completed the Bowes Railway.

As with many other County Durham and Teesside lines, much of the Bowes trackbed has been turned into a long-distance footpath and cycleway. The Bowes Railway Path runs between the Tanfield Railway at Marley Hill through Gateshead to Wardley, with a short detour around the heritage area of Bowes Railway at Springwell. From Wardley it continues as the Monkton Mineral Line through South Tyneside to Jarrow where it joins National Cycle Network route 14.

Tanfield

Maybe the best-known County Durham industrial line was the Tanfield Railway, which, as we saw in Chapter 1, dates back to 1647. Built as a wooden-railed horse-drawn waggonway, steel rails were installed in 1837, following an agreement with the new Brandling Junction Railway scheme and the Marquis of Bute, the owner of Tanfield Lea Colliery. It was converted to steam locomotive operation in 1881, when it became part of the national rail network after being acquired by the North Eastern Railway, although the self-acting inclines at Lobley Hill, Sunniside and Tanfield Moor were retained. Indeed, it is a rare example of a line that started out as a wooden waggonway and ended up as part of the main line system.

Predominantly used for mineral traffic, the Tanfield Railway also carried passengers, a service being introduced in 1842, but lasting only a few years. Marley Hill engine shed was

A typical private railway mineral working recreated on the Tanfield Railway, with 1943-built Robert Stephenson & Hawthorns' Austerity 0-6-0ST No 49 saddle tank at its head. This locomotive, which carries National Coal Board livery, was transferred to Backworth Colliery near Newcastle in 1959 and was preserved in 1976. (Brian Sharpe)

built in 1854, first being used to accommodate a stationary engine.

From 1945 onwards, the collieries along the line began to close down. When East Tanfield Colliery closed in 1964, so did most of the line. Marley Hill shed, however, remained in use until 1970, servicing locomotives for other collieries, while the bottom section of the line's branch at Redheugh served local factories until 1981. Austerity saddle tanks Nos 22 and 23 were the final engines at Marley Hill, and were scrapped there in 1971.

In the 1960s, when railway revival schemes were taking off elsewhere in Britain, the question was asked – why should County Durham, the cradle of the steam railway, not have a heritage line of its own?

The Tanfield Railway's Sir Cecil A Cochrane, *an 0-4-0 saddle tank, was built by Robert Stephenson & Hawthorns in 1948 and spent its entire working life at Redheugh gasworks in Gateshead, which stood alongside the bottom of the Tanfield branch. It was preserved in 1971. (Author)*

In 1971, in pursuit of such an aim, local enthusiasts moved into Marley Hill shed after the NCB moved out. Steam locomotive movements were taking place within two years, the first passenger rides taking place during a week in August 1975, and in 1977 the first stage of the heritage Tanfield Railway was opened from Marley Hill northwards to Bowes Bridge. The line was extended northwards to Sunniside in 1981, and in the 1990s, in stages, to Causey and East Tanfield, where the station was opened in 1997.

Meanwhile, a collection of industrial locomotives, both steam and diesel, was gradually being assembled as collieries, power stations and other commercial users closed down or modernised their internal system. The revivalists planned not to recreate a 'typical British Railways branch line' as was the case of other preserved railways, but one that reflected the ambience of the old independent railways of former years and the larger private lines that ran passenger trains. Thanks to the survival of Marley Hill shed so late in the day, the vintage machinery workshop is still capable of being used to overhaul locomotives.

Today's Tanfield Railway has superbly succeeded in its aim and alongside the Foxfield Railway in Staffordshire and the Chasewater Railway at Walsall, is one of Britain's finest industrial heritage railways.

Brandling Junction

The Brandling Junction Railway opened in 1839 from Gateshead with branches to Monkwearmouth and South Shields. An inclined plane ran down from Gateshead to Redheugh to join the Newcastle & Carlisle Railway, giving that line access to a coal staithe at Hillgate. The archway for the incline can still be seen in the 1906 King Edward VII railway bridge.

The Brandling Junction crossed the Stanhope & Tyne Railway at Pontop Crossing. It had a terminus in Broad Street, Monkwearmouth, while branches ran from Fulwell to North Dock on the River Wear, and to South Shields, following the Stanhope & Tyne Railway before turning towards the Tyne for the Brandling Drops. The railway was purchased by the Newcastle & Darlington Junction Railway in 1845 and much of the route between Gateshead and Monkwearmouth is now used by the Tyne and Wear Metro light rail system.

South Hetton

The South Hetton Railway opened in 1833 and was also known as Braddyll's Railway. It used rope haulage from South Hetton Colliery to Cold Hesleden Engine and then down to Seaham Harbour, with branches to Haswell Colliery and Murton Colliery. In the 1960s, coal from Eppleton, Elemore and Murton was sent underground to the new Hawthorn Combined Mine on the South Hetton Railway.

Ending a Durham legacy that began at Wylam Colliery in 1813, the South Hetton colliery line was the last place in the North East where steam locomotives were in daily commercial use. Three new diesels were bought from the North British Locomotive Company in 1969 to augment the existing steam fleet, but from 1973 onwards, modern traction began to replace steam locomotives, the last running three years later. The Seaham line's self-acting inclines were also the last of their type to be used in Britain, and the last incline of any type to work in the North East commercially, although in latter years they handled only washery waste.

South Hetton Colliery finally closed at Easter 1983, after a working life of 152 years. The railway built to serve it remained in place another two years – until it was destroyed during the miners' strike of 1984/5, by local people digging in the trackbed for coal. Following the demolition of South Hetton Colliery, the railway's locomotive sheds and workshops became unviable, and a replacement shed was opened at Hawthorn Combined Mine, part of Murton Colliery, with the private line serving them becoming unofficially known as Hawthorn Railways. In 1991 Murton Colliery and Hawthorn Combined Mine were closed, bringing to an end the history of private railways in Durham and the last section of the old Sunderland to Hartlepool and Durham railway network, which had stayed open for freight use, was dismantled.

Londonderry

The Londonderry Railway started as a wooden waggonway from the Londonderry pits to Penshaw Staithes, and was created by Charles Stewart, the powerful 3rd Marquis of Londonderry. For 35 years until his death on 6th March 1854, he dominated the Durham coal trade, laying down new railways and constructing a port and town at Seaham, building the harbour out into the sea. He employed John Buddle, who had been agent for the Lambton estates and its railway, in a similar capacity.

In 1827 the Duke of Wellington rode in a special carriage on the rope-hauled Londonderry Railway from Pittington Hallgarth via Benridge Bank Top and the Plain Pit to Colliery Row, where he examined a steam locomotive.

The Marquis had a five-mile private railway built between Seaham and Sunderland, opening in 1855 and also running public passenger services from 2nd July that year. George Hardy, who was placed in charge of locomotive repairs, eventually became the line's manager, a position he did not relinquish until his retirement in 1902 at the age of 77. In 1875 a private station on the line at Seaham Hall was built for the use of the family.

By 1860 the sprawling Londonerry Railway had reached its greatest extent, bringing coal from Framwellgate Moor, Shotton,

Steam lasted at Seaham Harbour, built by the Londonderry family, until the end of the 1960s. This 0-4-0 saddle tank, one of only a handful of locomotives constructed by steamboat builder Stephen Lewin of Poole, Dorset, was supplied new in 1877 to Seaham Harbour as a well tank and became the system's No 18. It was converted on site to a saddle tank in 1936 and withdrawn in 1969/70, before finding a permanent home at Beamish Museum where it ran for four years in the late 1970s. (Beamish Museum)

Teesside manufacturer Head Wrightson built 0-4-0 vertical-boilered tank engine No 33 'Coffee Pot' for use at Seaham Harbour, where it worked until 1962 as the docks' No 17. Its tiny proportions were perfect for working beneath the towering staithes on spilt coal reclamation and harbour breakwater maintenance work. It was displayed at the Stockton & Darlington Railway 150th celebrations at Shildon in 1975, and is now at Beamish Museum. (Beamish Museum)

Haswell and South Hetton into Seaham, and in 1865 engine and waggon workshops were opened at Seaham to serve it. However, from then on, the system began to contract. The Rainton & Seaham Railway, opened in 1831 to take coal from the pits at Londonderry pits to the then-new Seaham Harbour, burrowing under the Hetton Railway in the process, and using several inclined planes, closed as early as 1896.

From 1st October 1868, Londonderry trains were allowed to run into the North Eastern Railway's Hendon station, replacing the private line's Hebburn Burn station, and from 4th August 1879, into the then new Sunderland Central station itself, under powers obtained by the family, mainly for running trains for their own use.

In 1879 the Londonderry Railway took more than a million tons of coal to the staithes and docks at Sunderland, more than the NER carried there.

The 6th Marquis of Londonderry, backed by the NER, successfully opposed the building of a new Seaham to Hartlepool line. The NER subsequently bought the Londonderry Railway and took possession of it on 30th July 1890. In its final year of operation as an independent line, it carried more than 530,000 passengers.

The Londonderry Railway main line survives as Network Rail's Seaham–Sunderland line, but all of the independent company's branches are long gone. The collieries once owned by Londonderry Collieries Ltd, Vane Tempest, Seaham and Dawdon, have all closed. All rail traffic to Seaham Harbour ended in 1992 and the track was lifted, although a major cargo and distribution centre named CargoDurham was developed, with a new rail connection laid in 2001 along part of the Londonderry's Blastfurnace branch.

11

Dunston Staithes

This book may be about lost railways, but how can you lose what is claimed to be the biggest wooden structure in Europe?

The principal driving force behind virtually all of the railways in this volume was the conveyance of mineral traffic, often to the Tyne, the most important coal port in the North East. Large wooden piers, or staithes, for the purpose of loading minerals onto boats were constructed along the banks of the river, at Derwenthaugh, Wallsend, Jarrow, Tyne Dock, Blyth ... and Dunston, the biggest set of all.

The North Eastern Railway built Dunston Staithes in two stages. The first structure, which had three berths, was opened

The North Eastern Railway's gigantic Dunston Staithes back in the days of steamships. (Author's Collection)

in 1893; it was 1,725 ft long and stood 66 ft above the water line. A second and similar structure to the south followed in 1903, with a basin created out of the riverbank to service it.

The staithes extended more than 1,700 ft into the Tyne, running parallel to the riverbank before turning due south. A branch linked them to the Newcastle & Carlisle line at Norwood Junction. The staithes had several tracks running along the top of them. These tracks rose at a gradient of 1-in-96 from the western to the eastern end, allowing engines to shunt coal waggons to the correct height for loading ships anchored alongside the staithes. The waggons, which were fitted with trapdoors, were lined up with hoppers in the floor. Gangs of men known as 'teemers' would release these trapdoors so as to 'teem' the coal into the hoppers below. In turn, the hoppers were connected to coal chutes or 'spouts' and the teemers had to adjust these to the appropriate height for the ships being loaded, by use of a hand-operated windlass. Often, the coal would get jammed, and the teemers would jump in to free the coal, at great risk to themselves. Inside the ships' holds, other gangs of men called 'trimmers' levelled out the coal for stability.

In the 1920s Dunston Staithes shipped 140,000 tons of coal each week on ships destined for both London and the Continent. After the Second World War, the trade blockade forced countries to find fresh supplies of coal, and shipping from the staithes began to decline. By the 1970s just 3,000 tons of coal each week were passing through the staithes.

The North Staithes were finally closed after the final shipment on 4th March 1980, while the South Staithes were demolished. The branch line leading to them both was lifted.

The huge historical significance of Dunston Staithes was soon recognised, and they were restored and reopened for the Gateshead Garden Festival in 1990. Today, they are protected as a Listed Building and a Scheduled Ancient Monument.

Sadly, early on 20th November 2003, a section of the staithes was destroyed by fire. Public access onto the staithes is no longer

A view of the staithes today, with a middle section destroyed by fire. (Graham Soult/Creative Commons)

possible as a result, but they can be seen from the new riverside walkway opposite. In 2005 Gateshead Council commissioned a study into the possibility of the staithes' restoration.

12
Lost and Found: Museum Life

Beamish Museum and its J21
Monkwearmouth Station Museum

Beamish Museum and its J21

With the Durham coalfield depleted, it is highly unlikely that the likes of the hairnet-like mesh of railways that once carved up the county and Teesside will ever be seen again. Most of the winding routes built to tap rich mineral deposits, with passenger trains added to serve the mining communities that sprang up, will now remain firmly in the domain of lost railways. Yet it is still possible to step back in time and experience just what it was like in the days when railways revolutionised County Durham and then the world, and when industrialisation reached its zenith and few people had access to motor transport.

In short, the finest place to begin an exploration of lost railways is Beamish – the North of England Open Air Museum. Set in 300 acres of countryside, near to but not on several lost railway routes, it provides a stunning evocation of County Durham's transport of times past.

The 1825 Pockerley Waggonway, which features working replica locomotives from the dawn of railways, like the curious Steam Elephant and *Locomotion No 1*, has been laid on a decidedly green field site, just like the pioneer railways that carved up virgin countryside as coal pits and collieries mushroomed in the pastures and moorland alongside.

Jumping nearly a century, there is a short North Eastern Railway passenger line based on relocated Rowley station,

The coal loading plant at the Beamish colliery village. (Author)

designed to reflect life in the locality in 1913. A third railway recreates a typical colliery scene, with pithead waggons and sidings, based around a colliery village.

More recently a wooden-railed, early horse-drawn waggonway has been laid to complete a fuller picture.

The centrepiece of the museum is the town, where original Victorian buildings have been reassembled to create street scenes. You can visit the Annfield Plain Co-operative store, a terrace of professionals' houses from Gateshead, the Sun Inn from Bishop Auckland, a branch office of the *Sunderland Daily Echo*, a bandstand from Gateshead and even a Masonic Hall from Sunderland. Staff and re-enactors in period costume populate the shops and houses to explain their function to visitors.

You can travel round the huge site either on foot, by a regular vintage bus service, or by another form of railway, the street tram. A tramway forms a circuit of the site, calling at the town and the railway venues, and includes two vehicles from tram

151

Sunderland tram No 16 on the Beamish Museum tramway. (Author)

systems no longer with us – an enclosed double decker from Sunderland, No 16, which was built in 1900, and a Gateshead single decker, No 10, built in 1925.

Beamish took on its first two staff members in 1970 under the auspices of founder director Frank Atkinson, and the first exhibition was held in Beamish Hall in May 1971. The first tram entered service in 1973, and in July 1975 HM the Queen Mother visited the museum a month before it welcomed its 500,000th visitor. In September 1982 the British Rail chairman, Sir Peter Parker, took a footplate ride. Incidentally, he had arrived by train at the old Beamish station nearby, and was one of the last people to travel on the Consett line before it was taken up.

During four decades, Beamish Museum has, as might be expected, amassed a sizeable collection of railway artefacts from closed or modernised lines. And taking pride of place is a locomotive that, in the days of steam, was considered nothing special but today is regarded as being very special indeed.

The North Eastern Railway's C (LNER J21) class of 0-6-0 tender locomotives were in their day the workhorses of the railways of the industrial north-east, in particular on many of the lost lines featured in this book, such as the Stainmore route, where attempts to replace them with class D3 4-4-0s, D23 4-4-0s and E4 2-4-0s proved successful. The J21s, like the one in the cover painting, were arguably one of the most successful of the NER's locomotive classes.

Designed by the NER locomotive superintendent, Thomas William Worsdell, a total of 201 J21s were built between 1886 and 1894, and they became a trademark of the local railways, especially the branch lines. Although intended for mineral traffic, once fitted with train brakes, they were equally at home handling passenger services as freight.

The first withdrawals began in 1929 with No 1339, but at nationalisation on 1st January 1948 there were 83 still in service. Dieselisation finally put paid to them, with the last, No 65033, being withdrawn from service in April 1962. Before then, it had become a popular locomotive on enthusiasts' railtours covering now lost branch lines, including those run by the Railway Correspondence & Travel Society. On 7th May 1960 it hauled a

The sole surviving J21 0-6-0, No 65033, at Barnard Castle in British Railways days, is now the subject of a nationwide campaign to restore it as a living memorial to the lost railways of Durham. (Beamish Museum/Doug Hardy)

J21 No 65033 in its original North Eastern Railway livery at Beamish Museum. (Paul Jarman/Beamish Museum)

three-coach RCTS special over Stainmore, the last time a J21 would run over the legendary summit.

Yet No 65033 was a great survivor. Built in 1889, it had first been withdrawn on 22nd November 1939 as LNER No 5033, but due to wartime shortages had been repaired and returned to service! There are stories that it even hauled a 'special' taking Winston Churchill to Barnard Castle on 4th December 1942. After withdrawal by British Railways, it awaited the cutter's torch at Darlington for many years ... thankfully in vain, for it eventually found a new life in preservation, due to the perseverance of Frank Atkinson, who in May 1968 had it whisked away to Consett steelworks when told it was only days away from being cut up.

In 1970 the J21 was relocated to the Tanfield Railway, which then acted as a temporary home for some of the exhibits destined for Beamish. It was repainted into NER livery with its original number, 876, and returned to steam.

No 65033 ran at Beamish in July 1976 for the official opening of the museum's relocated Rowley station by poet laureate Sir John Betjeman, who wrote a poem to mark the occasion. The J21 remained in use at the museum until 1984, when it was withdrawn in need of a major overhaul, which experts have in recent years estimated will cost £500,000.

With no money available for such a project, No 65033 became one of the forgotten engines of preservation ... until a scheme was launched to rebuild it as a 'People's Engine'. While lacking the glamour and prestige of big-name locomotives like the *Flying Scotsman*, *Mallard* or *City of Truro*, far more than any of them it is the sole surviving example of a magnificent class that once made the Durham coalfield tick, and had a daily impact on the lives of everyone in the mining communities served by railways now long gone.

In 2009 the Locomotive Conservation and Learning Trust was set up to ensure a sustainable future for such railway artefacts, while at the same time promoting their educational value and supporting traditional skills. No 65033 was the first artefact placed in the Trust's care by Beamish Museum, along with NER bogie tools van No 5523, and a drive for public support and funding began in earnest. Trust chairman Julian Birley said: 'We will make a strong emphasis on not only restoring an engine, but also recapturing its history and trying to build a much bigger picture.'

At first moved to the North Norfolk Railway, where Julian is a director, No 65033 was subsequently moved back to home territory in County Durham, to the workshops at the Locomotion museum in Shildon where restoration, hopefully, will take place once sufficient money is available. When complete, it will tour heritage railways all over Britain, and may even make occasional main line journeys too. Through its restoration, the spirit of the lost railways of Durham and Teesside will be brought back to life to be enjoyed and appreciated by future generations. Further details about the project to rebuild No 65033 are available on the Locomotive Conservation and Learning Trust's website (www.ldt.org.uk).

Monkwearmouth Station Museum

Another museum that showcases Durham's railway heritage is Sunderland's Monkwearmouth Station Museum, which in the early 21st century underwent a £1 million refurbishment. The station, an outstanding Grade II listed building commissioned by railway entrepreneur George Hudson, was designed by Thomas Moore of Sunderland and opened in 1848 as the Sunderland terminus for Brandling Junction Railway trains from Gateshead and Newcastle.

Later superseded as the main station for the city, it closed to passengers in 1967 and was bought by Sunderland Corporation for conversion into a museum, including the restoration of the original booking office, which had remained unchanged since 1866. The Platform Gallery offers a view of the main line outside.

The museum, which outlines the history of travel and transport in Tyne and Wear, is owned by Sunderland City Council and managed on its behalf by Tyne & Wear Museums.

The classical frontage of Monkwearmouth station. (Tyne & Wear Museums)

INDEX